Sura | صورة

FRONT COVER

Pyramid complex of Senusret III at Dahshur

Marguerite Thirionet, the wife of Jean Capart, waves her arms on top of the pyramid of Senusret III during her first ever visit to Egypt. In the background, the Red Pyramid of Snefru is visible. The photo was taken during Capart's seventh voyage to Egypt, in 1927, during which he also excavated at Hiw on behalf of the Fondation Égyptologique Reine Élisabeth.

Jean Capart, between 25 January and 7 April 1927 (© RMAH, Inv. EGI.06169)

BACK COVER

Nile landscape

Egyptian villagers running along the bank of the Nile to greet Elisabeth, Queen of the Belgians, as her boat passes by. The photo was taken during the royal voyage of 1930, when the Queen travelled aboard the yacht *Khassed Kheir* of King Fuad I.

Jean Capart, 27 March 1930 (© RMAH, Inv. EGI.07034)

Sura | صورة

Egypt through a Belgian lens

Aude Gräzer Ohara, Athena Van der Perre, Marleen De Meyer & Wouter Claes

ROYAL MUSEUMS
OF ART AND HISTORY

snoeck

'My photos, if effective, shall reveal a real wonder'[1]

The Photographic Archive of the Egyptological Library
of the Royal Museums of Art and History, Brussels

In the morning, I spend an hour in the Luxor Temple, eagerly awaiting the moment when the lighting allows me to take a few photos. [...] From there, to the photographer's, where I'm delighted to see the excellent first results of my Bellieni, which continues to match its best performances.

— Jean Capart, 16 November 1945, in his personal travel diary

---

On the evening of 8 October 1945, Jean Capart embarked on what would be his last voyage to Egypt. The tension and excitement over this new journey, the first since 1938, is clearly palpable in his personal travel diary. His Bellieni stereo camera, Capart's most faithful travel companion, is once more carefully packed and kept close by his side. Already for more than four decades, it had served him to capture the monuments, landscapes and people of Egypt in thousands of photographs. Indeed, by the time Jean Capart wrote the above-quoted sentences in his travel diary, a vast collection of over 12,000 photographic glass plates[2] had been established at the Egyptological library of the Royal Museums of Art and History (RMAH) in Brussels. These photographs are predominantly the result of various missions to Egypt during which Jean Capart and his collaborators crossed the Nile Valley from the Mediterranean coast to its southern borders in Nubia. Study trips, archaeological excavations, royal voyages and official visits... the reasons behind these missions were diverse and manifold, but always with the underlying objective to develop and expand the photographic documentation of the museum's Egyptological library. Some voyages were even explicitly organised to bridge existing gaps in what today is an important and unique collection of historical photographs. It not only tells the story of this pioneering period of Belgian Egyptology, it also offers a kaleidoscopic view of a bygone Egypt, showing its dramatic landscapes, ancient monuments, archaeological expeditions and the diversity of its daily life.

PHOTOGRAPHY AND ARCHAEOLOGY

Since the invention of the daguerreotype process was announced in 1839, marking the beginning of modern photography, the countries of the Mediterranean basin and Egypt in particular played a pivotal role in the continued development of this new visual medium. Already in November of that same year, the Great Sphinx and the Pyramid of Khufu on the Giza Plateau, two of Egypt's most iconic and grandiose monuments, were captured through the lens of Horace Vernet and Frédéric Goupil-Fesquet.

---

1   Quote from Jean Capart's personal diary during a visit to the Royal Wadi and Royal Tomb at Amarna in 1930.
2   A detailed chronological inventory of this collection does not exist, but useful information on its development can be found in the annual reports of the Fondation Égyptologique Reine Élisabeth, published in their journal *Chronique d'Égypte*. In 1939, the collection of glass plates held around 11,700 items (Capart 1940: 14). In 1948, this number grew to about 12,600 (Werbrouck 1949: 5).

These images can be considered the first documented photographs of ancient Egyptian monuments.[3] Many other photographers followed in their footsteps and Egypt became a favourite destination of many early daguerreotypists. They were not only attracted by the grandeur of its pharaonic past or the country's exotic lure. The fact that sunny Egypt was blessed, particularly during wintertime, with favourable light conditions, essential for the lengthy exposure time of daguerreotypes, also played an important role. In the following decades, Egypt, along with Italy and Greece, served as an extensive practice ground where technical advances were tested, improved and diversified: shorter exposure times, easily prepared negatives that could be reproduced, and the invention of flash powder all contributed to a rapid development of photographic techniques.

Following these developments, Egypt became one of the world's most photographed countries and the steadily growing amount of photographs, published in books and newspapers or as postcards, all showing the richness of Egypt's cultural heritage and its people, resulted in swelling numbers of European and North American tourists who set off for a cruise upon the Nile. It is no understatement that mass tourism in Egypt was boosted and encouraged by photography and as such ushered in an era that is now commonly referred to as the 'Golden Age of Travel' (Humphreys 2014 and 2015).

While this 'commercial' aspect of photography certainly also stimulated the interest of historians, orientalists, philologists and last but not least archaeologists into Egypt's past, it also had a profound impact on the methodological framework of archaeology as a modern scientific discipline. Archaeologists rapidly understood the advantages of this new visual medium and, already in 1878, the first photographs of archaeological objects appeared in several articles published in Volume 2 of the *Bulletin de correspondance hellénique*. Prior to that, in 1854–1855, the Franco-American archaeologist and photographer John Beasley Greene had published two series of photographs of Egyptian monuments, of which the latter resulted from his excavations at Thebes (Greene 1854 and 1855). Around the same time, the eminent French Egyptologist Auguste Mariette, another early proponent of photography to the benefit of archaeological fieldwork, also made ample use of photography to document his important discoveries at the Saqqara necropolis.

Driven by the technical advances outlined above, which resulted, among other things, in the availability of easier-to-operate cameras and, more importantly, pre-treated glass plates, photography soon found itself at the very heart of archaeological methods and practices. Influential Egyptologists and archaeologists, such as James Henry Breasted, William Matthew Flinders Petrie and George Andrew Reisner, strongly advocated the use of photography[4] and by the early 20th century photographs were considered of crucial importance for empirically documenting the archaeological record.[5] To a certain degree, this epistemological shift revolutionised early modern archaeology and a photographic camera, operated by a proficient photographer, became as indispensable as the pencils of a skilled artist in documenting the archaeological process in all its facets.

THE BIRTH OF A UNIQUE PHOTOGRAPHIC COLLECTION: JEAN CAPART THE DOCUMENTALIST

At the end of the 19th century, a young ambitious Belgian scholar entered onto the international scene of Egyptology. By the age of 10, Jean Capart had already developed a true passion for ancient Egypt. Accompanied by his father, a physician regularly invited to speak at medical congresses abroad, he visited Egyptological collections in Europe's most important museums, such as the Louvre, the British Museum and the Egyptian Museum in Turin. For the sake of Egyptology, the young Capart also care-

---

3   Unfortunately, none of these original daguerreotype plates have stood the test of time. They were reproduced and survived as lithographs, which was a common practice in those days (Hüttner 2016: 12–13; Rammant-Peeters 1994: 243).

4   These three giants of Egyptian archaeology all wrote important contributions on the uses and practices of archaeological photography. See Breasted 1900; Petrie 1904: 73–84; for Reisner's unpublished manual on archaeological photography, see Der Manuelian 1992.

5   For a recent study on the interface between archaeology and photography and a critical review of the temporal complexity of photographs as a material archive, see McFayden & Hicks 2020 and Yelles 2020.

fully saved up his pocket money, allowing him to constitute a large personal library surpassing any other library in Belgium in terms of Egyptological scientific literature. With his appointment in 1901 as the first curator of the Egyptian collection at the RMAH in Brussels, Capart's dream to devote his life to the study of the monuments and documents of ancient Egypt came true.

Besides his desire and motivation to develop the museum's Egyptian collection and lend it international renown, Capart also lent great importance to the availability of all kinds of scientific and other documentation on both ancient and modern Egypt. This latter aspect runs as a connecting thread through his entire career and is reflected in different initiatives and projects, with some proving more feasible than others. Of highest priority in this respect was the development of an exhaustive Egyptological library. To this end, he donated his personal library to the museum shortly after his appointment in 1901. More than a thousand books and journals, including some of the most remarkable publications in the history of Egyptology, such as the *Description de l'Égypte* or Lepsius's *Denkmäler aus Ägypten und Äthiopien*, were added to the then modest museum library, which according to Capart contained hardly any serious Egyptological publications. Year after year, hundreds of books and journals were added to the collection and the library rapidly developed into one of the finest Egyptological libraries in the world. His donation also contained other types of documentation, such as more than 20,000 paper index cards, containing bibliographic and other information related to ancient Egypt, and over a thousand photographs that he collected or took himself. The availability of photographic documentation was another fundamental concern and priority for Capart, and in his view critical to executing his tasks as a museum curator and researcher. As a former student of Petrie, he recognised the interest and significance, as well as the possibilities, of photographic documentation. As such, he attached great importance to the continued development of not only the museum library, but also its photographic archives. Although Capart was not particularly successful as a field archaeologist, at least not until he started excavating at Elkab in 1937, he did cherish ambitions in that regard, particularly in the early years of his professional career. Yet, he quickly understood that this would not serve his aspirations to put the RMAH at the forefront of international Egyptology. Rather, collecting and centralising as much documentation as possible on ancient Egypt–while also making these documents accessible to researchers and laymen alike–seemed a better way of achieving this end.

Following the creation of the Fondation Égyptologique Reine Élisabeth (FÉRÉ) in 1923,[6] additional and substantial financial means became available and largely served Jean Capart's documentary ambitions, which he outlined in a presentation at the seventeenth International Congress of Orientalists at Oxford in 1928 (Capart 1928a). The library collection grew exponentially, the photographic archives were fed with thousands of photographs, and new documentary projects were initiated. A good example in this respect are the *fiches bibliographiques*, which were issued for the first time in 1935 and can be seen as laying the groundwork for the Annual Egyptological Bibliography.[7] Based on the official numbers published in the annual reports of the FÉRÉ, over 200,000 Belgian francs were spent on the acquisition or production of around 10,000 photographs and 6,000 glass plates between 1923 and 1933. All of this resulted in the creation of a unique study centre, for which the FÉRÉ and Jean Capart received much international acclaim, and effectively turned Brussels into a leading international centre of Egyptology in the 1930s.

PHOTOGRAPHING EGYPT

Within the photographic archives of the Egyptological library of the RMAH, the subcollection of photographic glass plates occupies a special place. Today, this collection comprises 14,277 individual items of great historic value. As already briefly outlined above, the vast majority of these photographs were taken by Capart and his collaborators during various trips to Egypt, where hun-

---

6   For more information on the history of the FÉRÉ, see De Meyer *et al.* 2023a.

7   The Annual Egyptological Bibliography was published between 1947 and 2001 and contained all possible references to Egyptological literature. Today it exists as an online database and is named Online Egyptological Bibliography, hosted by the Griffith Institute of Oxford University: https://oeb.griffith.ox.ac.uk/ (accessed 19/12/2022).

FIG. 1 The team of the Fondation Égyptologique Reine Élisabeth around 1930. Standing (from left to right): Marcel Hombert, Arpag Mekhitarian, Jean Capart and Sergei Miasnikoff; sitting (from left to right): Claire Préaux, Marcelle Werbrouck and Suzanne Berger (© RMAH, Inv. EGI-2.24397).

dreds of different monuments and archaeological sites were photographed. Capart travelled to Egypt thirteen times. Except for his first trip in 1900–1901, Capart always travelled in the company of other people, such as his second wife, Marguerite Thirionet, who joined her husband four times. On other occasions, he personally guided his friends of the American Goldman family or even the Belgian Queen Elisabeth during two of her visits to Egypt. Most of the time, however, he was in the company of one or several of his students and collaborators. Particularly worth mentioning in this respect are his former student Charles Mathien, and his collaborators at the museum and the FÉRÉ (FIG. 1): Éléonore Bille-de Mot, Arpag Mekhitarian, Baudouin van de Walle and Marcelle Werbrouck. Capart was not only their mentor in Egyptology, for he also instructed them in the intricacies of photography (Werbrouck 1947: 194).

Capart had a keen and patient eye for photography and mastered his Bellieni camera to perfection. Consciously aware of the perfect lighting conditions, he captured the subtleties of archaeological sites and monuments in an aesthetic manner. At the same time, his attention was not only drawn to the remains of Egypt's pharaonic past, for he was equally interested in the historical landscapes of the Nile Valley and even more drawn to the diverse traditions and customs of the Egyptian population. Although several unfortunately yet remain anonymous, the names and roles of many Egyptians featuring in his photographs are known. Based on research on the numerous documents kept in the archives of the RMAH and FÉRÉ, many of Capart's Egyptian co-workers, colleagues and friends are no longer nameless persons in a photograph, but they are recognised and acknowledged in their own right.

CONTENTS OF THE COLLECTION

'As I said earlier, the main outcome of our travels was the further enrichment of our photographic archives.'
— Capart 1928b: 9

The spirit of documentation that so permeated Capart's personality was a catalyst for the many voyages that he made during his lifetime. He went to Egypt, but also to many European and American collections, in order to build up what would become one of the largest photographic collections on ancient Egypt at the time. The contents of the photographic archive reflect this drive to document, with an eye for people, sites, landscapes and objects all mixed together. This is not to say that such images are neutral recordings of an unchangeable reality, as was aptly observed by Caraffa (2011: 24). Capart was an art historian, and these images were his way of collecting the world of (ancient) Egypt. The photographs should be seen as material objects, existing in a specific space and time, unable to escape the parameters within which they were created (see also Edwards & Hart 2004). This materiality of the photographs is further considered below, and the choice was made to print the glass negatives' black border, as well as the photo number inscribed upon them, as both constitute integral parts of the images as material objects. It is the only way in which the three-dimensionality of the photographs can somewhat be conveyed in the two-dimensional medium of a printed book. It should be noted that, in dealing with the archive and its digitisation, the recommendations of the Florence Declaration were observed.[8]

Excavations and travels

During his lifetime, Capart made thirteen voyages to Egypt, the first one in 1900–1901 and the last one in 1945–1946, close to his death in 1947. In this volume, photographs from nearly all these voyages are incorporated, about which a short overview is presented below with references to further literature. They cover the deployment of the museum's archaeological expeditions organised by both the RMAH and the FÉRÉ at Heliopolis (1907), Tell Hiw (1927) and especially Elkab (1937–1946). Many of these photographs had been forgotten and never previously published. In addition to documenting the progress of the excavations and the original find context of some 300 objects in the Egyptian collection of the RMAH originating from these excavations and surveys, there are also a remarkable number of photographs focusing on the Egyptian workmen, the local house staff, and life in the various villages in the immediate vicinity of Elkab. In combination with other archival documents kept at the RMAH, such as the original field diaries or the registers in which the salaries of the workmen and other expenses were recorded, they become visible in their own right as active collaborators in the process of knowledge production during the excavation seasons (De Meyer *et al.* 2023b).

These images also reflect Capart's extensive professional network. Several hundred photographs were taken by Capart and/or his collaborators of ongoing excavations conducted by the Service des Antiquités de l'Égypte and other institutions (universities, museums, and learned societies). In the overview below, only the excavations featured in this book are mentioned; therefore, not all active fieldwork projects figuring in the complete collection are here listed.

Overview of the voyages of Capart and his collaborators to Egypt

— December 1900–February 1901: First visit

During the winter of 1900–1901, Capart visited Egypt for the very first time, at the age of 23. Very few images of this trip are preserved in the collection of glass plate negatives: only ten are identified as such. However, he must have produced many more, since some were published in an article in which he shared his experiences and observations (Capart 1901). Capart focused his attention on the two major centres in the country: in the north, Cairo and its surroundings, to familiarise himself with ancient Memphis, and in the south, Luxor, to do the same for ancient Thebes. At Karnak, he visited the work of the French Egyptologist Georges Legrain on behalf of the Service des Antiquités de l'Égypte.

— November 1905–January 1906:
Expedition for the mastaba of Neferirtenef

Capart's second trip to Egypt was a true expedition, with the purpose to search for a chapel of an Old Kingdom mastaba tomb for the RMAH. After several attempts in the company of British archaeologist James E. Quibell, he finally settled on the mastaba of Neferirtenef, a 5th Dynasty official buried at Saqqara in the shadow of the Step Pyramid of Djoser (Bruffaerts 2005; Gräzer Ohara *et al.* 2023). The chapel was dismantled and the limestone blocks sent in individual crates to Brussels, where it was reconstructed in the museum in spring 1906. During this trip, Capart also visited many other sites, including the excavations of Édouard Naville at Deir el-Bahari (Egypt Exploration Fund). The entire operation, as well as the rest of his trip, is documented in more than 170 glass plate negatives.

— February–March 1907: Heliopolis

At the invitation of Belgian industrialist Baron Édouard Empain, Capart undertook his first archaeological expedition to Egypt in 1907 in the desert sand of Abbasiya, to the northeast of Cairo (Van Loo & Bruwier 2010; Bruwier & Doyen 2019). His student Charles Mathien and professor Fernand Mayence (Catholic University of Leuven) were also part of the team. They probed the ground, virgin territory at the time, for archaeological remains, before Empain constructed his new town of Heliopolis. No ancient vestiges were found in the area and Capart labelled himself a 'bad hunter'. The season is documented in almost 200 photographs.

---

8 'Recommendations for the Preservation of Analogue Photo Archives', 2009 https://www.khi.fi.it/en/photothek/florence-declaration.php (accessed 19/12/2022).

— March–April 1909: Abydos
The purpose of his 1909 voyage was to photograph the Temple of Seti I at Abydos, on which Capart published a monograph in 1912 (Capart 1912). At the invitation of John Garstang (University of Liverpool), who was working there at the time, he stayed ten days at the British Egyptologist's excavation house in the desert. This gave him the opportunity to spend a significant amount of time in the temple. In total, around 140 photographs of this trip are preserved in the archive.

— February–March 1923:
Tutankhamun with Queen Elisabeth
After the discovery of the tomb of Tutankhamun in November 1922, Queen Elisabeth of Belgium was determined to be present when the actual burial chamber was opened in February 1923 (Capart 1923; Bruffaerts 1998). She travelled to Egypt with her son, Crown Prince Leopold, and Jean Capart as her guide. In the wake of this visit, the group also embarked upon a Nile cruise, stopping at many sites. The 116 photographs in the archive complement other photographic archives of this trip, notably those at the Royal Palace in Brussels, where the Queen's personal photo albums are preserved.

— April 1925: Study trip with students
In 1925, Capart represented Belgium at the Eleventh International Geographical Congress, held in Cairo from 1 to 9 April, the first post-war congress of its kind. He took along his oldest daughter, Elisabeth, as well as several of his students: Éléonore Bille-de Mot, Marie Weynants-Ronday, Daisy Goldschmidt and Denyse Vaes. The group was joined by Marcelle Werbrouck and Baudouin van de Walle in Cairo. Together they visited sites and museums in Alexandria, Cairo, Middle Egypt and the wider Luxor area. More than 200 glass plate negatives of this trip were added to the collection.

— January–March 1927: Tell Hiw
From 14 to 20 February, the FÉRÉ team carried out an archaeological campaign at Tell Hiw in Upper Egypt (Capart 1927). Accompanied by several of his collaborators, this was also the first trip to Egypt that Capart's wife Marguerite Thirionet made. She is featured in several of the nearly 200 photographs of this voyage preserved in the archive.

— January–March 1929: Photographic mission
In 1929, Jean Capart travelled to Egypt with one specific mission: photographing objects in the Egyptian Museum of Cairo, as well as monuments and sites in the Memphite area hitherto underrepresented in the photographic archives (Capart 1929). He also went to Upper Egypt, where he visited the excavation sites of several French and American colleagues. Of this trip, almost 100 glass plates have been preserved.

— January–April 1930: Goldman family & royal voyage
The greater number of glass plate negatives in the collection originate from the 1930 trip. This is not surprising, since Capart in fact made two back-to-back voyages through Egypt from north to south (Bruffaerts 2006). The first one was a Nile cruise with the American Goldman family aboard the S.S. Fostat (see image #190), a Thomas Cook steamer, from early January until early March (Capart 1930a). Immediately thereafter, he joined the state visit of King Albert I and Queen Elisabeth of Belgium to Egypt, after which he accompanied the Queen during her Nile voyage (Capart 1930b) (FIG. 2). King Albert took that opportunity to fly to Baghdad. Some 250 photographs document the Goldman trip, while about 100 were taken during the second royal voyage. Capart also visited Robert L. Mond's excavations at Armant (Egypt Exploration Society), among many others.

— December 1933–February 1934: Amarna
As advisory curator at the Brooklyn Museum, Capart convinced Brooklyn to contribute financially to the Egypt Exploration Society mission to Amarna, under the direction of John D.S. Pendlebury. In January 1934, he travelled there together with his wife Marguerite Thirionet and several of his collaborators (Capart & Werbrouck 1934). He stayed for nearly two weeks at the British excavation house, documenting the archaeological work and making excursions to different sites in Egypt. He for instance paid a visit to the French missions at Tanis in the Delta (directed by Pierre Montet) and at Tod in Upper Egypt (directed by Fernand Bisson de la Roque). The archive preserves over 325 glass plate negatives of this trip.

— February–March 1937: Elkab, first mission
The first Elkab campaign took place during February–March 1937, led by Jean Capart and a small group of his collaborators: Marcelle Werbrouck, Arpag Mekhitarian,

FIG. 2 Queen Elisabeth of Belgium and Jean Capart at the granite quarries in Aswan, photographed by Paul Polinet on 29 March 1930 (© RMAH, Inv. EGI.07557)

Éléonore Bille-de Mot and Violette Verhoogen. The architect Jean Stiénon also joined the team at the recommendation of Art Nouveau pioneer Victor Horta. The foreman (*reis*) of the Egyptian workmen was Chared Mohammed Mansur. During that first season of fieldwork, the Belgian team concentrated its efforts on the temples of Nekhbet and Thoth within the great enclosure wall.[9] The archive holds almost 150 photographs of this season.

— January–March 1938: Elkab, second mission
During the second Elkab campaign led by Jean Capart, fieldwork continued in the same area of the Nekhbet and Thoth temples, but also expanded beyond the temples-proper. Participants were Marcelle Werbrouck, Marcelle Baud and Jean Stiénon. This season is documented in 109 photographs. The onset of the Second World War compromised plans for a third campaign in 1939.

— November 1945–February 1946:
   Elkab, third mission
Only after the war did Capart manage to return to Elkab once more. His team consisted of Marcelle Werbrouck, Arpag Mekhitarian, Adhémar Massart and Jozef Janssen. During this season, work expanded beyond Elkab-proper, and the small pyramid at el-Kula was also investigated archaeologically. Other archaeological missions visited included those directed by Émile Baraize at Deir el-Bahari for the Service des Antiquités de l'Égypte. This was Capart's last excavation season and final stay in Egypt, as he would pass away one year later on 16 June 1947. Of this season, 164 photographs are preserved in the archive.

These images document the state of preservation and conservation, as well as the setting and landscape, of a vast array of monuments and sites spread across the entire Nile Valley. As several elements in the Egyptian landscape have profoundly changed since the early 20th century—due to expanding agriculture, construction works (e.g. the Aswan High Dam in the 1960s), and the growth of settlements driven by an exponentially increasing population—these photographs have become ever more valuable.

Museum objects

Apart from photographing the country and the remains of its past, Capart also wanted to create a concise overview of the material culture preserved in museums. He was well-connected with the international community of Egyptologists, and often visited his European, Egyptian and American colleagues. This network allowed him to expand the collection of museum object photos beyond the objects preserved in Brussels. Between 1900 and 1939, Capart frequently received permission from his superiors to travel to England, in order to visit the annual exhibitions with objects from the British excavations in Egypt carried out by such organisations as the Egypt Exploration Fund/Society, the British School of Archaeology in Egypt, and the Liverpool Institute of Archaeology. During these trips, he photographed hundreds of objects from Egyptian collections at the local museums. His personal notebooks and diaries, several of which are kept at the RMAH, frequently provide additional information on the objects he photographed. When Capart was not able to photograph certain objects himself, he contacted museum curators with the request for object photos in order to enrich the Brussels collection. Several museums willingly fulfilled this request and provided extensive series of object photos, made by their own staff, such as the Louvre in Paris, the Ashmolean in Oxford, the Ny Carlsberg Glyptotek in Copenhagen, the National Museum of Antiquities in Leiden, the Archaeological Museum in

---

9 For an overview of Belgian fieldwork at Elkab, see Limme 2008. A popularising book that Capart wrote following the 1945–1946 season summarises work and life at Elkab during the three excavation campaigns (Capart 1946).

Bologna, and the Museum August Kestner in Hanover. In some cases, the name of the colleague who took the actual photos in the cooperating museum is preserved, such as Miss Else Grantz, who photographed hundreds of objects from the Egyptian collection of the Berlin Museum in 1928 on Capart's behalf (Capart 1928b: 9–10).

Even though Capart's photographic project enjoyed wide support within the international Egyptological scene, not all curators were willing to grant his wishes. The keeper of the Oriental Department of the British Museum, E.A. Wallis Budge, was not keen on providing photos to Capart, nor did he give him permission to photograph certain objects himself. In one of his travel reports, Capart furiously condemned the 'hostility of the curator Budge towards all scientific work in his department'.[10] This difficult relationship explains why the majority of object photos from the British Museum were purchased from the collection of W.A. Mansell, who published several catalogues of object photographs from the British Museum at the end of the 19th century.

The international allure of the collection was further heightened when Capart toured the USA between 1924 and 1925 as Visiting Professor, at the invitation of the Commission for Relief in Belgium Educational Foundation. He lectured at 44 universities and institutions across the country, and combined this with visits to several Egyptian collections. Capart's American tour had several direct consequences for the RMAH. A large donation of photos from the Metropolitan Museum of Art in New York, including more than 200 images of objects from the collection of Lord Carnarvon, arrived in Brussels in 1928 (Capart 1928b: 10). In 1932, Capart was appointed advisory curator at the Brooklyn Museum, in charge of the development of its Egyptian collection, and up until the outbreak of World War II he divided his time between Brussels and Brooklyn. During these years, the Brussels collection was enlarged with photos of the objects at Brooklyn, but also at other American institutions, such as the Museum of Fine Arts in Boston and the New York Historical Society.

It is not surprising, given these international contributions, that the entire collection of museum object photos current-

FIG. 3A A branch of a sycamore tree (*Ficus sycomorus*) with figs from the island of Roda, photographed by Ludwig Keimer on 7 June 1929
(© RMAH, Inv. EGI.07794)

FIG. 3B Ludwig Keimer in a sycamore tree, photographed on 7 June 1929
(© RMAH, Inv. EGI-2.07970)

---

10   Travel report written by Capart to Eugène van Overloop, 04/08/1907, Archives RMAH, dir. 61/31: Rapport voyage en Angleterre 1907.

ly comprises some 3,200 glass plate negatives and covers objects from Egyptian collections on three continents.

Flora and fauna

A small but important subcollection of the photographic archive concerns a set of images produced by German Egyptologist Ludwig (Louis) Keimer in the late 1920s and early 1930s (Lehnert 2023). After the death of his mentor Georg Schweinfurth in 1925, he left Germany for Egypt. Keimer had a strong interest in Egypt's flora and fauna, which was further stimulated by Capart. In exchange for an annual allowance, Keimer provided the RMAH with photographic documentation on Egypt's botanical and animal heritage. As such, Keimer disposed of additional means to pursue his research, and Capart was able to further develop and enrich the photographic archive with a new subject matter that previously had not received much attention from the Egyptological community. This three-year contract ran from 1929 until 1932, and Keimer published several articles in the *Chronique d'Égypte*.[11] He was especially interested at that time in the sycamore tree, on which he was preparing a monograph that however would never be published (FIG. 3). He also undertook a study trip to the Delta to investigate the lotus (*Nelumbium speciosum*, FIG. 4). In addition to photographs, he also collected small antiquities, objects depicting animals and plants, that he sold to the RMAH.

THE MATERIALITY OF THE PHOTOGRAPHS

The collection of glass plate negatives housed at the Egyptological library of the RMAH consists of more than 14,000 items, of which the oldest date back to 1901 when Jean Capart made his first trip to Egypt, and the most recent to the 1955 excavations at Elkab, directed by Pierre Gilbert (1904–1986). From a technical point of view, the majority of the glass negatives are normal plates and monograms. Approximately one quarter of the images were taken with a Bellieni stereo camera (see below) on 9 × 8 cm glass plates, of which at least 3,200 form 1,600 stereo pairs (FIG. 5).

In order to use these images to illustrate lectures and classes, which was an important objective of the collection, pos-

FIG. 4A A lotus bud (*Nelumbium speciosum*) rising up in a pond (© RMAH, Inv. EGI.07827)

FIG. 4B A lotus flower (© RMAH, Inv. EGI.07829)

FIG. 5 Stereophotograph of the monumental gate of Sheshenq III in the temple of Amun at Tanis, photographed by Jean Capart in 1934 (© RMAH, Inv. EGI.10025)

---

11 For instance: Keimer 1931.

FIG. 6A The wooden cabinets in which the glass lantern slides are preserved in the Egyptological library of the RMAH, c. 1930 (© RMAH, Inv. EGI-2.21543, photographer unknown)

FIG. 6B The same wooden cabinets today (photo M. De Meyer)

FIG. 6C Detail of the drawers (photo W. Claes)

itive projection slides were made of them, also on glass and also stored at the museum in wooden cabinets (FIG. 6). On these lantern slides, handwritten labels were added with the photo number and a brief description of the image (FIG. 7). At the same time, an index was kept in two paper index card catalogues, organised by inventory number or geographical location. However, the information on the old index cards was highly fragmentary and far from standardised. Therefore, in the SURA project, new metadata was researched and added for each image. These lantern slides went everywhere that Capart went to deliver talks, to the general public, to students, and at scientific gatherings.

In 1928, Capart described in detail the progress and the process of dealing with the photographic collection. This passage makes clear that the collection was composed of both images taken by Capart and his collaborators during their voyages, and commercially produced glass slides purchased from museums around the world and from photographic establishments such as Seif & Gaddis at Luxor.

> *A few years back, we possessed some two thousand photographs, many of which were taken during my travels through Egypt and in the museums of Europe since 1899. We have since added over three thousand photos, including a thousand from the excellent Seif & Gaddis series and five hundred. […]*
>
> *From Berlin, we brought back more than a hundred photographs, many specially taken for the Foundation by Miss Grantz, whose talent and obligingness are deserving of praise. Hildesheim and Leyde gave us precious documents. Leipzig and Hanover have promised us images. […]*
>
> *New York has already sent us over two hundred objects from the Carnarvon Collection; I shall receive some four hundred more. […] The programme for Boston includes around a hundred photographs, including a few of the mastabas' reliefs to be made specially for us.*
>
> *We are expecting photos from Oxford, Cambridge, Copenhagen and Hamburg. We have acquired the entire series of Egyptian documents from the 'Photographic Archives of Art and History' in Paris.*

FIG. 7A Glass lantern slides with their labels inside the cabinet
(photo M. De Meyer)

FIG. 7B Selection of glass lantern slides (© RMAH)

Upon their arrival in Brussels, all of these photographs are numbered, listed in a register, categorised and indexed on cards. For this long work, Miss Werbrouck has found an assistant as intelligent as she is dedicated in Miss E. de Mot.

At the same time, and prior to their final classification, the photographs of the most important items are sent to the museum studio, where projector slides of them are made. A thousand new plates have thus been added to our collections, the richness of which becomes daily more apparent for the preparation of classes and conferences.

— Capart 1928b: 9–10

Thus, many of the photographs that Capart bought or obtained from colleagues as prints, were photographed and converted into lantern slides. FIG. 8 shows an example of a print of a photograph by Antonio Beato, while FIG. 9 is a print of a set of aerial views of Egypt made by Theodor Kofler in 1914.[12] Illustrations in Egyptological publications that were deemed essential for lectures were also photographed. On several of the images can be seen the contraptions used to facilitate this process, ranging from tags for fixing prints to a wooden board (FIG. 8-9), to metal slats for holding down the sides (FIG. 10-12), to more elaborate constructions like an easel for photographing large publications upright (FIG. 13) or for instance plaster casts of relief fragments (FIG. 14).

In rare instances, these images give a hint of the products used at the time; for instance, in FIG. 15 can be seen a box of 'Hauff Diapositiv Platten' (12 plates of 8.5 × 10) bought at 'Photographie optique Maison S. Gecelle D. Avanzo Succ. Bruxelles'. In FIG. 16, four boxes of glass projector slides (Agfa Gevaert and Guilleminot) hold down the pages of a book. And in FIG. 17, two hands hold up a book with its pages flattened between a wooden board and a glass sheet, with the book also resting upon a box of German glass plates from the company Mimosa AG in Dresden.

While dealing with glass plates at the museum already entailed considerable logistics, things proved much more complicated out in the field in Egypt, where the heavy plates needed to be purchased at specialised stores, then carried around and developed locally (FIG. 18). Capart regularly commented on such matters, as when he wrote in his diary on 12 February 1930: 'I have received the first photos from Lehnert: twenty boxes with generally very good results. [...] I will have the negatives and prints sent to Brussels, which will facilitate the classification work.' During the long voyage on the Nile with the Goldman

---

12   For more on Kofler's aerial photos, see Piacentini 2014 and 2015.

FIG. 8 Print of a photograph by Antonio Beato of a striding statue of Amenhotep III usurped by Ramesses II at the Luxor Temple (© RMAH, Inv. EGI.02471)

FIG. 10 The Elkab workmen photographed by Jean Stiénon in 1937. This image shows two prints mounted together on a wooden board and then rephotographed in order to create a landscape effect (© RMAH, Inv. EGI.11411)

FIG. 9 Aerial view of the Luxor Temple made by Theodor Kofler in 1914 (© RMAH, Inv. EGI.00097)

FIG. 11 Jean Capart poses on the base of a standing colossal statue of Amenhotep III or Horemheb at the temple of Karnak, photographed by Queen Elisabeth in 1923 (© RMAH, Inv. EGI.02994)

FIG. 12 Collection of cat statues from Sheikh Ibada/Antinoöpolis in the collection of the RMAH (© RMAH, Inv. EGI.05713)

FIG. 14 Photograph of a plaster cast of a New Kingdom relief preserved in the Musée du Louvre in Paris; photographer and date unknown
(© RMAH, Inv. EGI.02828)

FIG. 13 Photograph of plate 11 published in Calverley, Amice & Broome, Myrtle F. 1935. *The Temple of King Sethos I at Abydos, Volume II: The Chapels of Amen-Rē', Rē'-Ḥarakhti, Ptah, and King Sethos*, London, The Egypt Exploration Society; Chicago, The Oriental Institute of the University of Chicago. The drawing, made by Amice Calverley, shows King Seti I offering to the sacred barks of Amun-Re, Mut and Khonsu; photographer unknown, after 1935
(© RMAH, Inv. EGI.01552)

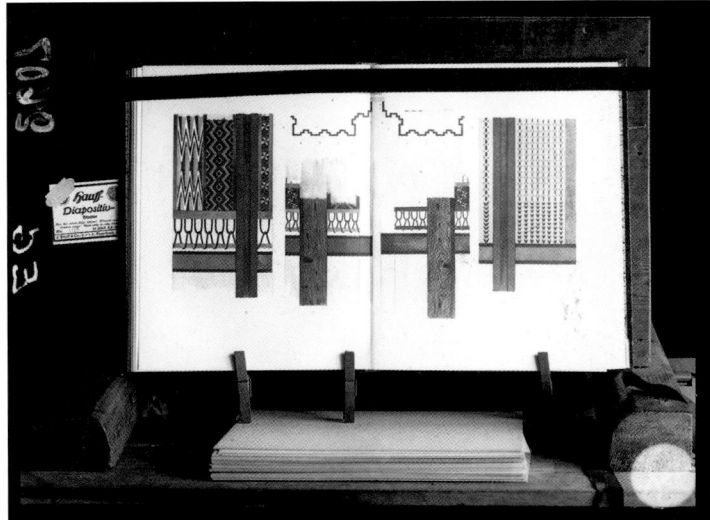

FIG. 15 Photograph of plate 8 published in Quibell, James Edward. 1913. *Excavations at Saqqara (1911–12): The Tomb of Hesy*. Cairo, Service des Antiquités de l'Égypte. A box of 'Hauff Diapositiv Platten' is used to prop up the volume; photographer unknown, after 1913
(© RMAH, Inv. EGI.02607)

FIG. 16 Photograph of plate 88 published in Cassas, Louis François. 1799, *Voyage pittoresque de la Syrie, de la Phénicie, de la Palestine et de la Basse-Egypte*. Paris, s.n. The drawing shows the Old Kingdom rock-cut tomb of Debehen in the Khafre quarry cemetery at Giza. Four boxes of glass projector slides (Agfa Gevaert and Guilleminot) are used to hold the pages down (© RMAH, Inv. EGI.04270, photographer unknown)

FIG. 17 Photograph of plate 4 published in Lauer, Jean-Philippe. 1936. *La pyramide à degrés 1 : l'architecture*. Cairo, Imprimerie de l'Institut Français d'Archéologie Orientale. The image shows a reconstruction drawing of the Step Pyramid complex of Djoser at Saqqara; photographer unknown, after 1936 (© RMAH, Inv. EGI.11012)

family, he ran out of glass plates in Aswan. On 23 February 1930, he wrote: 'I am taking advantage of the break to go make two stereoscopic photos at the obelisk in the quarry. These are my last plates. The provision ordered by dispatch has yet to arrive!' On 3 March, he announced, 'I am taking to Lehnert the final plates for developing.' The shop he twice refers to is Lehnert & Landrock, one of the oldest photography stores in Cairo that still exists today.[13]

CAPART'S BELLIENI STEREO CAMERA

The camera that Capart carried with him everywhere he went in Egypt, was a Bellieni stereo camera. He often refers to the camera himself, and in his obituary Marcelle Werbrouck observes how inseparably connected the two were:

> *Of each of them, there remains at the Foundation, as a sincere and eloquent testimony, that of his inseparable Bellieni jumelle. For our master in Egyptology was also our master in photography, and his projector slides truly captured the soul of Egypt.*
>
> — Werbrouck 1947: 194

---

13 For a brief history of Lehnert & Landrock, see https://egyptswiss.wixsite.com/yehia/lehnert-and-landrock (accessed 19/12/2022).

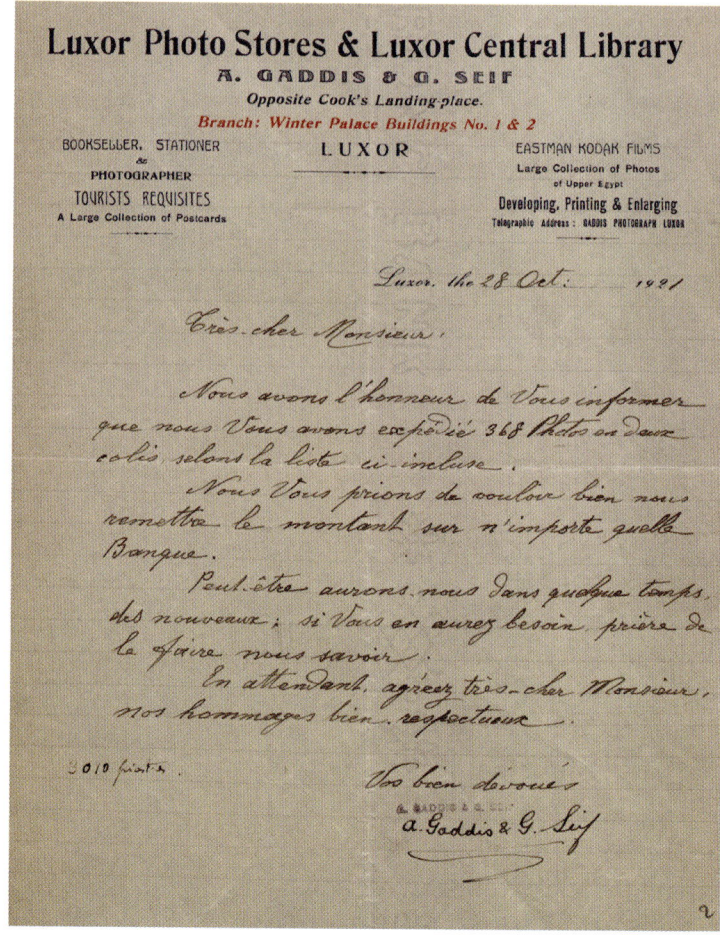

FIG. 18 Letter from A. Gaddis & G. Seif (photo store in Luxor) confirming the order of photographic prints by Capart, 28 October 1921 (© RMAH)

FIG. 19 Capart taking a photograph with his Bellieni camera in the desert at Abydos; still from a film made by the Goldman family in 1930
(© Theodore Lehmann, courtesy of Harvard University)

FIG. 19 shows Capart taking a photograph with this Bellieni stereo camera in the desert of Abydos in 1930, while image #145 shows him using it in Medinet Habu that same year. Although the bag he used for carrying his glass plates is preserved at the RMAH (FIG. 20), his camera had long since vanished. However, it recently resurfaced thanks to the power of media. The SURA project was featured on the RTBF news of 27 January 2021, in which it was mentioned that his camera had been lost. Soon afterwards, we were contacted by Ms Annelie Campion from Brussels, stating she owns that very camera (FIG. 21). She and her husband run a camera store and collect vintage and classic cameras. Many years ago, her husband gifted her with Capart's camera, sold to him by one of Capart's grandchildren. In addition to a documented history confirming the Bellieni's authenticity, a small ivory label affixed to the camera and mentioning 'Docteur Capart–5, Rue d'Egmont, 5–Bruxelles' confirms that the camera originally belonged to Jean Capart's father, the medical doctor Alphonse Capart.

SURA PROJECT

The importance of the photographic collection of the RMAH was internationally acknowledged during the first half of the 20th century, but at some later point the Egyptological community was no longer aware of its content and in some ways even of its existence. The lack of interest resulted in neglect, despite its great historical value, and the images of the pioneering years of Belgian Egyptology, as well as Capart's photographic skills fell into oblivion. In 2020, to remedy this situation, the SURA project[14] was launched, as a collaboration between the RMAH and Egyptologists from KU Leuven (Gräzer Ohara *et al.* 2021; Van der Perre *et al.* 2021). In keeping with Capart's original ambition, the objective of the SURA project ('sura' meaning 'photo' in Arabic) was to study and digitally share this collection with the international scientific community and the general public alike.

The combination of the previous housing conditions at the museum and the decades-long neglect, led to traces of chemical and biological degradation in some glass plates. In order to preserve this collection for future generations, immediate action was required. As a first step, the entire collection was digitised in high resolution at the Royal Observatory of Belgium, using state-of-the-art technology initially developed for the digitisation of astro-photographic plates. Digitising stellar images on glass plates necessitates the creation of a high-precision digital dataset, and using the same facilities for this collection allowed for the creation of high-quality, incredibly detailed digital imagery.

Once this step was completed, a long-term preservation plan was established and specific conservation measures were taken, including repacking the glass plates in acid-free cases and individual envelopes. To avoid further irreversible damage, the glass plates are now stored in a protective, climate-controlled environment.

The main goal of the SURA project was to catalogue the digitised images in the RMAH's central collections management system[15] together with new metadata. Besides each image's technical information (dimensions, type of photo, state of preservation), this required a description of its contents. The second step was therefore a critical revision of the available (meta)data for each individual im-

---

14 www.sura-project.be (accessed 19/12/2022).
15 https://www.carmentis.be/eMP/eMuseumPlus.

FIG. 20 The bag for carrying the photographic glass plates, preserved at the RMAH (photo M. De Meyer)

FIG. 21 Capart's Bellieni stereo camera in the possession of Ms Annelie Campion (photo M. De Meyer)

age, consisting of the handwritten label on the (positive) glass plate and two paper index card catalogues. These cards only contained very limited information, such as a place, a date or the photographer's name. Detailed information on the specific (parts of) monuments, their orientation, or the names of persons appearing in the photographs was lacking, and even basic information on the photographic framework (photographer, date) was not always given. The SURA team complemented the available metadata with as much additional information as possible. For this research, the archives of the RMAH proved a true goldmine, as they contain valuable sources, such as Capart's personal notebooks, diaries, letters, etc. In a subsequent phase, these references will be made available as cross-links with the RMAH's online library and archival catalogue, including access to the electronic versions of publications and archival material when possible.

Images of objects stored at the RMAH are also cross-linked to these objects in the museum's online catalogue. In the future, this will be expanded, when applicable, to the online catalogues of other museums, thus recreating Capart's international network in the digital world.

The project's intentions extend beyond simply making these images available online. The archival and database research led for instance to new insights in the search for the mastaba of Neferirtenef (RMAH E.02465), uncovering new information on the original location of the mastaba at Saqqara, and on all mastabas declined by Capart before his finally selecting this one (Gräzer Ohara *et al.* 2023). Another research track concerned the Egyptian workmen (Quftis and local workmen from the Elkab area), who worked with Capart's team at Elkab and are featured in numerous photographs (De Meyer *et al.* 2023b).

AN ANTHOLOGY OF IMAGES

> *While he set great store by the authority of his words, he also recognised, certainly more than anyone else, the power of images and the need to illustrate his presentations with photos as perfect as possible. These he chose with great care, never satisfied with a mediocre or poor document.*
> — De Keyser 1947: 210

For Capart, visual documentation was just as important as the written kind, and he combined the two in a way that may seem self-evident in today's visually-oversaturated world, but which was certainly not the case back in the first half of the 20th century. While he never could have read Susan Sontag's 1970s collection of essays *On Photography*, he would have subscribed to her vision in the opening lines of her essay 'In Plato's Cave':

> *Humankind lingers unregeneratively in Plato's cave, still revelling, its age-old habit, in mere images of the truth. But being educated by photographs is not like being educated by older, more artisanal images. For one thing, there are a great many more images around, claiming our attention. The inventory started in 1839 and since then just about everything has been photographed, or so it seems. This very insatiability of the photographing eye changes the terms of confinement in the cave, our world. In teaching us a new visual code, photographs alter and enlarge our notions of what is worth looking at and what we have a right to observe. They are a grammar and, even more importantly, an ethics of seeing. Finally, the most grandiose result of the photographic enterprise is to give us the sense that we can hold the whole world in our heads—as an anthology of images.*
> — Sontag 1970: 3

The more than 200 images reproduced in this book are only a minor selection of the grand archive described above, through which the FÉRÉ team attempted to hold the world of ancient and modern Egypt in their heads. They have been selected based on a combination of subject matter and aesthetic considerations. The choice to study this collection at this point in time is not arbitrary. It coincides with other initiatives examining the development of Egyptology in its specific Belgian context, with strong ties to royalty and industry in the first half of the 20th century. The project 'Pyramids and Progress: Belgian expansionism and the making of Egyptology, 1830–1952' (De Meyer *et al.* 2019) is a multidisciplinary project uniting modern historians, Egyptologists and archivists from five Belgian institutions (universities and museums). One result of this project was the publication of a popular biography of Jean Capart (Bruffaerts 2022), also illustrated with images from the glass plate archive under study in the SURA project. In March–October 2023, the RMAH hosts an extensive exhibition entitled 'Expedition Egypt', which addresses the development of Egyptology in Belgium from the 19th century up until today. Here too images from the collection will be featured. These are just a few examples of the concerted efforts made by the small country of Belgium to critically investigate the genesis of this discipline, while in so doing not shying away from confronting its own colonial past (Vanhulle 2023).

ORGANISATION OF THE BOOK

> *The systematic listing of the photographs classified by geographic order or by categories of ideas, shall redouble the value of our documentation.*
> — Capart 1932: 6

The geographic organisation of his photographic collection, on which Capart mused in 1932, would never be realised in his lifetime. Even today, the projection slides are still in the order in which they were left decades ago. But in this book, the images are presented in geographic order, taking the reader on a journey up the Nile in the footsteps of Capart and his collaborators, from their arrival at the port of Alexandria, to the fortified site of Semna in modern Sudan, the southernmost point of their travels. All sites mentioned in the book are indicated on the map on the adjoining page.

Every image is accompanied by a short description and, when available, information on the photographer and date. In some cases, diary entries by Capart or preserved correspondence has made it possible to establish the image's exact date. Sometimes the information on the image's original paper index card was meagre, and further archival research only resulted in connecting the photo to a particular year. The same holds true for the identification of people shown in these photographs. Thanks to the diaries and the archives, not only Capart's relatives and collaborators, but also many of his Egyptian friends and colleagues could be identified and acknowledged.

Not all names and terms mentioned in this book are familiar to non-Egyptologists. Therefore, a glossary is provided on p. 234, with brief background information on the persons mentioned, as well as definitions of the (ancient) Egyptian and Arabic words used. This glossary also serves as an index, with references to the photo numbers in the book.

Timeline of Ancient Egyptian History

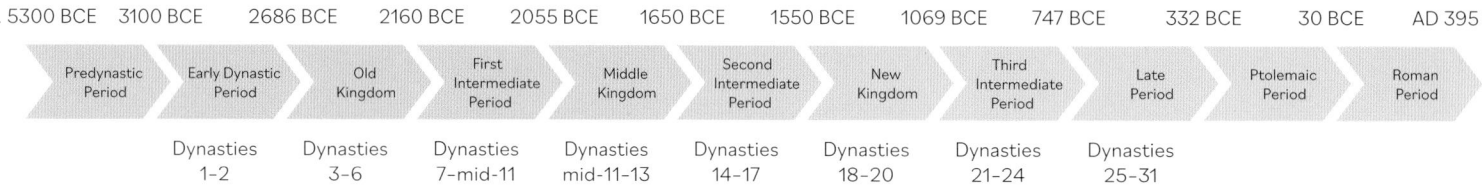

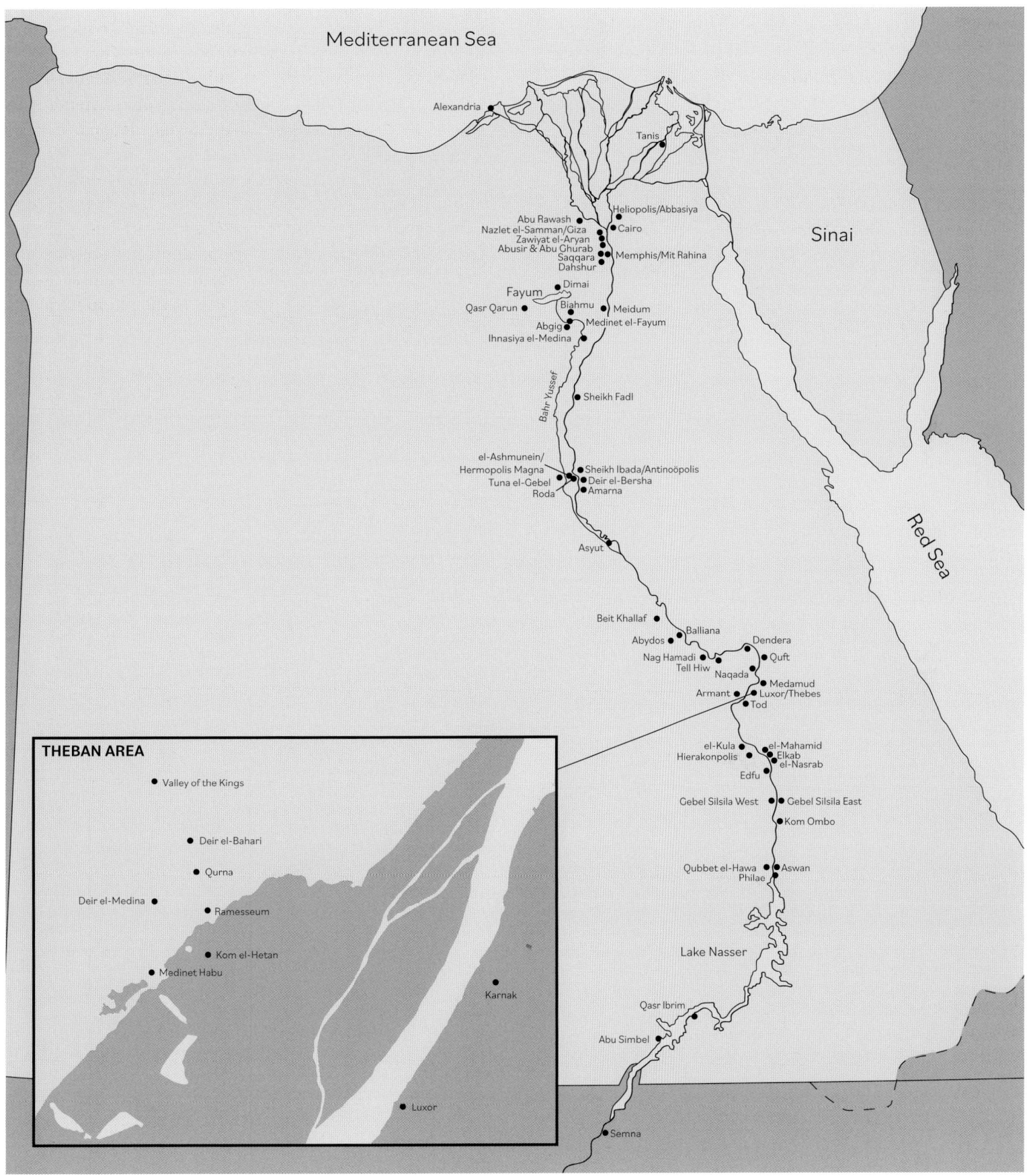

قام بزيارة مجموعات الآثار المصرية في كبريات المتاحف الأوروبية، مثل متحف اللوفر والمتحف البريطاني والمتحف المصري في تورينو. ونظرًا لهوايته بعلم المصريات، عني كابارت الفتى بادّخار مصروف جيبه لتشكيل مكتبته الشخصية الضخمة التي فاقت أي مكتبة أخرى في بلجيكا من حيث ما تضمّنته من الأدبيات العلمية في مجال المصريات. وبتعيينه عام 1901 كأول أمين للمجموعة المصرية في المتحف الملكي للفن والتاريخ ببروكسل، تحقّق حلمه بتكريس حياته لدراسة الآثار المصرية القديمة وتوثيقها.

وإلى جانب رغبة كابارت وهمّته في تطوير مجموعة الآثار المصرية في المتحف وإيصالها للشهرة العالمية، أولى أهمية بالغة لتأمين جميع أنواع الوثائق العلمية وغير العلمية عن مصر القديمة والحديثة. وشكّل ذلك مسارًا تواصل طوال حياته المهنية وانعكس في مختلف المبادرات والمشاريع التي ثبت أن بعضَها أكثر جدوى من بعضها الآخر. وتمثلت الأولوية القصوى لديه في تطوير مكتبة شاملة للمصريات. وتحقيقا لهذه الغاية، تبرّع بمكتبته الشخصية للمتحف بعد فترة وجيزة من تعيينه في عام 1901. وبهذا أضاف إلى مكتبة المتحف المتواضعة آنذاك، والتي كادت لا تحتوي على أية منشورات جدّية في علم المصريات، أكثرَ من ألف كتاب ومجلة، بما فيها عدد لا بأس به من أبرز المنشورات في تاريخ علم المصريات، مثل موسوعة «وصف مصر» وكذلك «معالم أثرية من مصر وأثيوبيا» لكارل ريتشارد ليبسيوس. وعامًا بعد عام، أضيفت مئات الكتب والمجلات إلى المكتبة التي تطورت بسرعة لتصبح واحدةً من أرقى مكتبات المصريات في العالم. وتضمّن تبرعُه أيضاً أنواعًا أخرى من الوثائق، كمجموعة من أكثر من عشرين ألف بطاقة فهرسة ورقية تحتوي على معلومات بليوغرافية وغيرها من المعلومات المتعلقة بمصر القديمة، وأكثر من ألف صورة جمعها أو التقطها بنفسه. وشكّل توفر الوثائق الفوتوغرافية أحدَ الاهتمامات والأولويات الأساسية الأخرى لدى كابارت الذي رأى فيها أمرًا بالغ الأهمية لتنفيذ مهامه كأمين متحفي وباحث. وكونُه من قدامى طلاب مائيو فليندرز بيتري جعله يدرك فائدة وشأن التصوير الفوتوغرافي والإمكانيات التي أتاحها. وبهذا اهتم اهتمامًا كبيرًا بالتطوير المستمر ليس فقط لمكتبة المتحف، ولكن أيضاً لأرشيفها من الصور الفوتوغرافية. وعلى الرغم من أن كابارت لم يكن ناجحًا في العمل الآثاري الميداني، على الأقل حتى بدئه بالتنقيب في مدينة الكاب في عام 1937، إلّا أنه كان يُضمِر طموحًا في هذا الصدد، لا سيما في السنوات الأولى من حياته المهنية. ولكنه سرعان ما فهم أن ذلك لن يخدم تطلعاته لوضع المتحف الملكي للفن والتاريخ في طليعة علم المصريات على الصعيد الدولي؛ وأنّ الطريقة المثلى لتحقيق هذه الغاية إنّما تكمن في جمع أكبر قدر ممكن من الوثائق عن مصر القديمة في مركز واحد، وجعلها في متناول الباحثين والعامة على حد سواء.

وفي أعقاب إنشاء مؤسسة الملكة إليزابيث لعلم المصريات في عام 1923[6]، توفّرت الموارد المالية الإضافية الوافرة، وخدمت إلى حد كبير طموحات جان كابارت التوثيقية التي حدّدها في عرض تقديمي أدلى به أمام المؤتمر الدولي السابع عشر للمستشرقين في أكسفورد عام 1928 (كابارت 1928a). وبهذا نمت مجموعة المكتبة نموًّا مطردًا، وأُثرَيت الأرشيفات الفوتوغرافية بآلاف الصور، وأُطلقت المشاريع التوثيقية الجديدة؛ خير مثال على ذلك، البطاقات البليوغرافية التي صدرت لأول مرة في عام 1935 وتُعَدّ بمثابة الأساس للبليوغرافيا المصرية السنوية[7]. وبناءً على الأرقام الرسمية الواردة في التقارير السنوية للمؤسسة، أنفق أكثر من مائتي ألف فرنك بلجيكي على اقتناء وإنتاج حوالي عشرة آلاف صورة فوتوغرافية وستة آلاف لوح زجاجي بين عامي 1923 و1933. فأسفر كل هذا عن نشوء مركز دراسي فريد من نوعه نالت عنه المؤسسة وجان كابارت إشادة دولية واسعة، ما جعل بروكسل قطبًا دوليًّا رائدًا في علم المصريات إبّان ثلاثينيات القرن العشرين.

تصوير مصر

تحتل المجموعة الفرعية لألواح التصوير الزجاجية مكانةً خاصة ضمن الأرشيفات الفوتوغرافية في مكتبة المصريات بالمتحف الملكي للفن والتاريخ. وهي تضم اليوم 14.277 عنصرًا فرديًّا وتتمتع بقيمة تاريخية عظيمة. وكما تم توضيحه بإيجاز آنفًا، التُقطت الغالبية العظمى من هذه الصور على يد كابارت ومعاونيه خلال رحلاتهم إلى مصر، حيث صوّروا المئات من المعالم والمواقع الأثرية. لقد سافر كابارت إلى مصر ثلاث عشرة مرة؛ وباستثناء رحلته الأولى في 1900-1901، كان يسافر دومًا بصحبة أشخاص آخرين، مثل زوجته الثانية مارجريت ثيريونيت التي انضمت إليه أربع مرات. وفي مناسبات أخرى، قام شخصيًّا بدور المرشد لأصدقائه من عائلة جولدمان الأمريكية أو حتى لملكة بلجيكا إليزابيث خلال زيارتين من زياراتها إلى مصر. ولكنه في معظم الأوقات كان يسافر بصحبة واحد أو أكثر من طلابه ومعاونيه. وتجدر الإشارة هنا بشكل خاص إلى تلميذه السابق تشارلز مائيان، ومعاونيه في المتحف ومؤسسة الملكة إليزابيث للمصريات (الشكل1): إليونور بيل-دي موت، أرباخ مختياريان، بودوين فان دي فال، مارسيلا فيربروك. ولم يكن كابارت معلمهم في علم المصريات فحسب، بل علّمهم كذلك تقنيات التصوير الفوتوغرافي وتعقيداته (فيربروك 1947: 194).

لقد كان كابارت حريصًا وصبورًا على التصوير الفوتوغرافي وأتقن العمل على كاميرته من موديل بيليني إلى حد الكمال. ونظرًا لمعرفته العميقة بظروف الإضاءة المثالية، أفلح في التقاط أدقّ التفاصيل للمواقع والمعالم الأثرية بطريقة جمالية. وفي الوقت ذاته، لم يلتفت فحسب إلى أطلال الماضي الفرعوني، بل اهتمّ بالقدر نفسه بالمناظر الطبيعية التاريخية لوادي النيل، وبالتقاليد والعادات المتنوعة لدى المصريين. وعلى الرغم من أن الكثيرين من المصريين في صوره لا يزالون مجهولين للأسف، إلّا أننا استطعنا التعرّف على أسماء بعضهم ووظائفهم بفضل الوثائق المحفوظة في أرشيفات المتحف الملكي ومؤسسة علم المصريات، التي سمحت بتحديد هويات زملاء كابارت والعاملين معه وأصدقائه المصريين ووظائفهم وعلاقتهم به وبمعاونيه، فلم يعودوا مجرّد أشخاص مجهولين في الصور.

محتويات المجموعة

كما سبق وذكرتُ، تمثّلت النتيجة الرئيسية لرحلاتنا في إثراء أرشيفات الصور الفوتوغرافية لدينا.

(كابارت 1928b: 9)

تمتعت شخصية كابارت برغبة جامحة في التوثيق شكّلت حافزًا قويًّا للرحلات العديدة التي قام بها خلال حياته. فقد ذهب إلى مصر، ولكنه زار أيضًا مختلف المتاحف الأوروبية والأمريكية للاطّلاع على مجموعاتها المصرية، من أجل تشكيل ما سيصبح إحدى أكبر مجموعات الصور الفوتوغرافية عن مصر القديمة في ذلك الحين. وتعكس محتويات أرشيف الصور الفوتوغرافية ذلك الدافع للتوثيق، مع التركيز في الوقت نفسه على الناس والمواقع والمناظر الطبيعية والقطع الأثرية. ولكن هذا لا يعني أن هذه الصور، كما لاحظ كارافًّا (2011: 24)، كانت مجرّد تسجيل محايد لواقع ثابت لا يتغيّر. فجان كابارت كان أيضًا مؤرّخًا للفن، وكانت تلك الصور طريقته في التقاط العالم المصري (القديم)، وينبغي أن يُنظر إليها على أنها أشياء مادية وُجدت في مكان وزمان محدّدين، ولا يمكنها الإفلات من الظروف التي صُنعت فيها (انظر أيضًا: إدواردز وهارت، 2004). وسنتطرّق أدناه باستفاضة إلى مفهوم الأهمية المادية الذاتية للصور الفوتوغرافية. وقد ارتأينا طباعةَ الصور السلبية الزجاجية مع أظهرها السوداء وأرقام الصور المنقوشة عليها، من حيث إن الإطار والرقم يُشكّل كلاهما جزءًا لا يتجزأ من الأهمية المادّية للصورة. فهذه هي الطريقة الوحيدة التي يمكن من خلالها نقل الصور ثلاثية الأبعاد إلى السطح ثنائي الأبعاد في الكتاب المطبوع. وتجدر الإشارة إلى مراعاتنا لتوصيات إعلان فلورنسا في التعامل مع الأرشيف ورقمنته[8].

الحفريات والرحلات

خلال حياته، قام كابارت بثلاث عشرة رحلة إلى مصر، كانت الأولى في 1900-1901 والأخيرة في 1945-1946 قبل وفاته بقليل في عام 1947. وفي هذا الكتاب، أُدرجت صورٌ من جميع هذه الرحلات تقريبًا، مرفقةً بلمحة موجزة وبالمزيد من المراجع ذات الصلة. وهي تغطي البعثات الأثرية التي نظمها كلٌّ من المتحف الملكي ومؤسسة المصريات في هليوبوليس (1907)، وتل هو (1927)، والكاب على وجه الخصوص (1937-1946). وكان الكثير من هذه الصور قد طواها النسيان ولم تُنشر من قبل؛ وهي توثّق التقدم في الحفريات وتحدّد أماكن العثور على 300 قطعة منتمية إلى المجموعة المصرية بالمتحف الملكي، استُخرجت خلال تلك الحفريات والمسوحات الأثرية. فضلًا عن ذلك ثمة عدد لا بأس به من الصور التي تركّز على العمال المصريين والعاملين المحليين في منازل البعثات، والحياة اليومية في مختلف القرى المحاذية للكاب. وباقتران الصور مع الوثائق الأرشيفية الأخرى المحفوظة في المتحف الملكي، كدفاتر اليوميات الميدانية الأصلية وسجلات رواتب العمال والمصروفات الأخرى، صار لهؤلاء الناس وجودٌ بحد ذاتهم بصفتهم مساهمين فاعلين في عملية إنتاج المعرفة أثناء مواسم التنقيب (دي ماير وآخرون 2023b).

---

6. للحصول على المزيد من المعلومات عن تاريخ مؤسسة الملكة إليزابيث لعلم المصريات، انظر دي ماير وآخرون 2023a.
7. صدرت البليوغرافيا المصرية السنوية بين عام 1947 وعام 2001، وتضمنت كافة المراجع الموجودة على الانترنت تحت تسمية «البليوغرافيا المصرية أونلاين»، ويستضيفها معهد جريفيث بجامعة أكسفورد: https://oeb.griffith.ox.ac.uk (الدخول في 19/12/2022).
8. توصيات بشأن حفظ أرشيفات الصور الفوتوغرافية النظرية، 2009 https://www.khi.fi.it/en/photothek/florence-declaration.php (الدخول في 19/12/2022).

«إنْ نجحتْ الصورُ التي التقطتُها، فستكشف عن العجائب»[1]

الأرشيف الفوتوغرافي لقسم المصريات
في المتحف الملكي للفن والتاريخ ببروكسل

عند الصباح، قضيتُ نحو ساعة في معبد الأقصر، منتظرًا بفارغ الصبر اللحظة التي ستسمح الإضاءةُ فيها بالتقاط بعض الصور [...]. ومن هناك أسرعتُ إلى مختبر التصوير حيث اعترانى السرور باكتشاف الصور الأولى الممتازة لكاميرتي من موديل بيليني، والتي كانت لا تزال تُتحفني بأفضل النتائج.

(جان كابارت، 16 نوفمبر 1945، في يوميات رحلاته)

في مساء الثامن من أكتوبر 1945، انطلق جان كابارت في رحلته التي ستكون الأخيرة إلى مصر. ويتّضح من يوميات رحلاته مدى تحمّسه وتشوّقه لهذه الرحلة الجديدة، الأولى له منذ عام 1938. وقد عَني بتوضيب كاميرته بيليني مزدوجة العدسات (ستريو)، رفيقة أسفاره الوفية، وحرص على إبقائها بالقرب منه. فقد خدمته لأكثر من أربعة عقود في التقاط آلاف الصور للآثار والمناظر الطبيعية والناس في مصر. وفي واقع الأمر، بحلول الوقت الذي كتب فيه جان كابارت الكلمات الواردة آنفًا في يومياته، كانت مكتبة علم المصريات بالمتحف الملكي للفن والتاريخ ببروكسل قد أثريت بمجموعة كبيرة من أكثر من اثني عشر ألف لوحة زجاجية فوتوغرافية[2]. وكانت هذه الصور في غالبيتها ثمرةً لمختلف البعثات إلى مصر التي اجتاز خلالها جان كابارت وفريقُه وادي النيل من ساحل البحر المتوسط إلى حدود النهر الجنوبية في النوبة. وقد تنوّعت المسوّغات الكامنة من وراء هذه البعثات وتشعّبت، كالرحلات الدراسية والحفريات الأثرية والرحلات الملكية والزيارات الرسمية؛ ولكن هدفَها الرئيسي تمثّل دومًا في تطوير وتوسيع الوثائق الفوتوغرافية في مكتبة علم المصريات بالمتحف. وهناك عددٌ من الرحلات نُظّم تحديدًا لسد الثغرات في ما أصبح اليوم مجموعة عظيمة واستثنائية من الصور التاريخية، التي لا تروي فقط قصة تلك الفترة الرائدة في علم المصريات البلجيكي، بل تعطي كذلك نظرات متعددة عن مصر الغابرة، ومناظرها الطبيعية الدرامية، وآثارها القديمة، والحياة اليومية فيها، والبعثات الأثرية التي ترددت عليها.

من تصوير الصروح العظيمة إلى توثيق السجلات الآثارية

منذ الإعلان عن اختراع التصوير على الألواح الفضية (داجيروتايب) في عام 1839، إيذانًا ببداية التصوير الفوتوغرافي الحديث، لعبت بلدان حوض البحر المتوسّط على وجه العموم، ومصر على وجه الخصوص، دورًا محوريًا في التطور المستمر لهذه الوسيلة البصرية الجديدة. وبالفعل، في نوفمبر من ذلك العام نفسه، التقطت عدساتُ المصوّرَين هوراس فيرنيه وفريدريك جوبيل-فيسكيه صورًا لتمثال أبي الهول وهرم خوفو على هضبة الجيزة، وهما من أكثر المعالم شهرة وعظمة في مصر. وتُعدّ تلك الصور أول الصور الفوتوغرافية الموثّقة للآثار المصرية القديمة[3]. وسار على هذه الخطى العديدُ من المصورين الأوائل وصارت مصر وجهتهم المفضلة، وجذبتهم ليس فقط لعظمة ماضيها الفرعوني وسحرها غير المألوف، ولكن أيضًا نظرًا لشمسها، وبخاصة في فصل الشتاء، التي أتاحت شروط الإضاءة الملائمة لمدد التعرّض الطويلة التي تطلّبها التصويرُ على الألواح الفضية (داجيروتايب). وعلى مدى العقود التالية، أصبحت مصر وإيطاليا واليونان ميدانًا واسعًا لممارسة التصوير جرى فيه اختبار التقدم التقني وتحسينه وتنويعه: كتقصير مدد التعرض، وتبسيط كيفية إعداد الصور السلبية القابلة للنسخ، واختراع مسحوق الفلاش؛ ما أسهم في التطور السريع لتقنيات التصوير الفوتوغرافي.

وفي أعقاب هذه التطورات، أصبحت مصر أحدَ البلدان الأكثر تصويرًا في العالم. وأظهر الكمُّ المتزايد للصور الفوتوغرافية المنشورة في الكتب والصحف والبطاقات البريدية، ثراءَ التراث الثقافي لمصر وشعبها، مما أسفر عن تعاظم أعداد السياح من أوروبا وأمريكا الشمالية الذين تهافتوا على الرحلات النهرية في النيل. وليس من قبيل المبالغة أن نقول أن التصوير الفوتوغرافي هو الذي عزّز السياحة الجماهيرية في مصر وشجّعها، إيذانًا بما دُعي «العصر الذهبي للسفر» (همفريز 2014 و2015).

ومن المؤكد أن هذا الجانب التجاري، إن صح التعبير، للتصوير الفوتوغرافي قد استرعى أيضًا اهتمام المؤرخين والمستشرقين وعلماء اللغة والآثاريين بماضي مصر، وترك أثرًا عميقًا على الإطار المنهجي لعلم الآثار كونه فرعًا علميًا حديثًا. فسرعان ما أدرك الآثاريون مزايا هذه الوسيلة البصرية الجديدة؛ ولم يحلّ عام 1878 إلّا وقد ظهرت أولى الصور للقطع الأثرية في المقالات الواردة في العدد الثاني من «نشرة المراسلات اليونانية» الصادرة عن المدرسة الفرنسية بأثينا. وقبل ذلك، في 1854-1855، كان عالم الآثار والمصور الفرنسي الأمريكي جون بيسلي جرين، قد نشر سلسلتين من الصور الفوتوغرافية للآثار المصرية، التُقطت السلسلة الثانية منها خلال حفرياته في طيبة (جرين 1854 و1855). وفي الوقت نفسه تقريبًا، كان عالم المصريات الفرنسي البارز أوجست ماريت من أوائل المؤيدين لاستخدام التصوير الفوتوغرافي في العمل الآثاري الميداني، واستفاد استفادة واسعة منه لتوثيق اكتشافاته المهمة في مقابر سقّارة.

وقد سمح التقدم التقني المذكور أعلاه بتوفير الكاميرات سهلة التشغيل والألواح الزجاجية المعالَجة مسبقًا. ونتيجةً لذلك، سرعان ما دُمج التصوير الفوتوغرافي في صميم المنهجيات والممارسات الآثارية. ودافع عنه بقوة كبارُ علماء المصريات والآثاريين، من أمثال جيمس هنري برستد، ووليام مايو فليندرز بيتري، وجورج أندرو رايزنر[4]، واكتست الصور الفوتوغرافية في أوائل القرن العشرين أهميةً حاسمة في التوثيق التجريبي للسجلات الآثارية[5]. وأحدث هذا التبدّل المعرفي ثورةً في علم الآثار الحديث في أيامه الأولى، وأصبحت الكاميرا الفوتوغرافية التي يُشغّلها المصور المحترف، أداةً لا غنى عنها لتوثيق العمليات الآثارية من جميع جوانبها، كأقلام الرصاص في يد الفنان الماهر.

نشأةُ مجموعةٍ فوتوغرافية استثنائية: جان كابارت الموثّق

عند نهاية القرن التاسع عشر، ولج إلى الساحة الدولية لعلم المصريات باحثٌ بلجيكي شاب وطموح هو جان كابارت، الذي شُغف شغفًا كبيرًا بمصر القديمة منذ كان في العاشرة من عمره. فبرفقة والده الطبيب الذي دُعي للمحاضرة في المؤتمرات الطبية في الخارج،

---

1. اقتباس من يوميات كابارت الشخصية خلال زيارته لوادي الملوك ومقابر العمارنة الملكية عام 1930.
2. ليس هناك جردٌ مفصّلٌ متسلسلٌ زمنيًا لهذه المجموعة، ولكن يمكن العثور على معلومات مفيدة عن تطورها في التقارير السنوية لمؤسسة الملكة إليزابيث لعلم المصريات والصادرة في مجلتها «وقائع مصرية». في عام 1939، تضمنت مجموعة الألواح الزجاجية نحو 11700 عنصر (كابارت 1940: 14). وفي عام 1948، ازداد هذا العدد ليصل إلى نحو 12600 (فيبروك 1949: 5).
3. للأسف لم يصمد أيٌّ من ألواح «داجيروتايب» الأصلية هذه أمام اختبار الزمن. ولكنها كانت قد استُنسخت في المطبوعات الحجرية كما كان شائعًا في تلك الأيام (هوتر 2016: 12-13؛ رامانت-بيترز 1994: 243). [بالفلمنكية: رامانت-بيترز 1994: 6؛ بالفرنسية رامانت-بيترز 1994: 191]
4. كتب هؤلاء العمالقة الثلاثة في ميدان علم الآثار المصرية إسهامات مهمة حول استخدامات وممارسات التصوير الفوتوغرافي الأثري. انظر آل برستد 1900؛ بيتري 1904: 73-84؛ وبشأن كتيّب رايسنر غير المنشور عن التصوير الفوتوغرافي الأثري، انظر دير مانويليان 1992.
5. للاطلاع على دراسة حديثة عن التلاقي بين علم الآثار والتصوير الضوئي، وعلى مراجعة نقدية للتعقد الزمني للصور الفوتوغرافية بصفتها مادة أرشيفية، انظر مكفايدن وهيكس 2020 وييلز 2020.

— يناير – مارس 1938: البعثة الثانية في الكاب

خلال البعثة الثانية في الكاب تحت إشراف جان كابارت، استمر العمل الميداني في نفس المنطقة من معبدَي نخبت وتحوت، لكنه امتد أيضًا إلى ما وراء المعابد. وشارك في هذه البعثة مارسيلا فيربروك ومارسيلا بود وجان ستينون. وجرى توثيق هذا الموسم في 109 صور. ثم أدى اندلاع الحرب العالمية الثانية إلى عرقلة التخطيط للبعثة الثالثة التي كان من المزمع إجراؤها في عام 1939.

— نوفمبر 1945 – فبراير 1946: البعثة الثالثة في الكاب

توجّب على كابارت انتظار نهاية الحرب لكي يتمكن من العودة إلى الكاب مرة أخرى. وتألّف فريقُه من مارسيلا فيربروك، أرباج مخيتاريان، أدمار ماسارت وجوزيف يانسن. وتوسع العمل خلال هذا الموسم إلى ما وراء الكاب، وأجريت دراسة آثارية للهرم الصغير في الكولا. ونُظّمت زيارات لعدد من البعثات الأثرية الأخرى من بينها البعثة التي كان يشرف عليها إميل باريس في الدير البحري لصالح قطاع الآثار المصرية. وقد كان هذا آخر موسم تنقيب لكابارت ورحلته الأخيرة إلى مصر، إذ وافته المنية بعد عام واحد في 16 يونيو 1947. وقد احتُفظ بنحو 164 صورة في الأرشيف من هذا الموسم.

وتُوثّق هذه الصورُ حالة حفظ وصون عدد كبير من المعالم والمواقع المنتشرة عبر وادي النيل بأكمله، فضلًا عن بيئاتها والمناظر الطبيعية المحيطة بها. ونظرًا للتغيرات العميقة التي طرأت في مصر منذ مطلع القرن العشرين - كالتوسع في الزراعة وأعمال البناء (مثل السد العالي في أسوان في ستينيات القرن العشرين)، والتمدد العمراني نتيجةً للتضخم السكاني المظرد، صارت هذه الصور تكتسي أهمية أكثر من أي وقت مضى.

القطع الأثرية في المتحف

فضلًا عن تصوير مصر وأطلال ماضيها، أراد كابارت تشكيل نظرة عامة موجزة عن الآثار المحفوظة في المتاحف. وكان على تواصلٍ جيد مع أوساط علماء المصريات الدولية، وغالبًا ما كان يزور زملاءه الأوروبيين والمصريين والأمريكيين. وقد سمحت له هذه الشبكة من العلاقات بتوسيع مجموعة صور المتحف للقطع الأثرية بما يتجاوز القطع المحفوظة في بروكسل. وبين عامي 1900 و 1939، كثيرًا ما حصل على أذونات من رؤسائه للسفر إلى إنجلترا من أجل زيارة المعارض السنوية التي تضمّنت القطع الأثرية المكتشفة خلال الحفريات البريطانية في مصر التي أجرتها مختلف الجهات، مثل صندوق/جمعية استكشاف مصر والمدرسة البريطانية للآثار بمصر ومعهد ليفربول للآثار. وأثناء هذه الرحلات، قام بتصوير مئات القطع الأثرية من المجموعات المصرية في المتاحف المحلية. وسجّل الكثير من المعلومات الإضافية حول القطع التي صوّرها في دفاتر ملاحظاته ويومياته الشخصية المحتفَظ بالعديد منها في المتحف الملكي للفن والتاريخ. وعندما لم يكن قادرًا على تصوير القطع بنفسه، اتصل بأمناء المتاحف طالبًا صورَها من أجل إثراء مجموعة بروكسل. وقد لبّت العديد من المتاحف هذا الطلب من طيب خاطر وزوّدته بسلاسل واسعة من صور القطع الأثرية التي التقطها موظفوها، مثل متحف اللوفر بباريس، ومتحف أشموليان بأكسفورد، وني كارلسبرغ غليبتوتيك بكوبنهاغن، والمتحف الوطني للآثار في ليدن بهولندا، والمتحف الأثري في بولونيا بإيطاليا، ومتحف أوغست كيستنر في هانوفر. وقد حُفظت أسماء بعض الزملاء الذين التقطوا الصور في المتاحف المتعاونة، مثل الآنسة إيلزا جرانتز التي صورت نيابة عن كابارت مئات القطع الأثرية من المجموعة المصرية في متحف برلين عام 1928 (كابارت 9-10 :1928b).

وعلى الرغم من أن مشروع كابارت للتصوير الفوتوغرافي قد حظي بدعم واسع في الأوساط الدولية لعلم المصريات، فإن أمناء المتاحف لم يكونوا جميعًا على استعداد لتلبية رغباته. فأمين قسم الآثار الشرقية في المتحف البريطاني إرنست ألفرد واليس بودج، لم يرغب بتزويده بالصور ولم يمنحه الإذن بتصوير قطع معينة بنفسه. وفي تقرير إحدى رحلاته، أدان كابارت بشدة «عداء بودج تجاه جميع الأنشطة العلمية في قسمه»[10]. وتفسّر هذه العلاقة الصعبة سببَ شراء غالبية صور القطع الأثرية الموجودة في المتحف البريطاني من مجموعة مانسيل الذي نشر عدة كتالوجات لصور القطع الأثرية ضمن مجموعة المتحف البريطاني عند نهاية القرن التاسع عشر.

ازدادت جاذبيةُ مجموعة الصور على الصعيد الدولي عندما قام كابارت بجولة في الولايات المتحدة الأمريكية بين عامي 1924 و 1925 كأستاذ زائر بدعوة من المؤسسة التعليمية التابعة للجنة الإغاثة في بلجيكا. وحاضَر في أربع وأربعين جامعة ومؤسسة في جميع أنحاء البلاد، وزار العديدَ من مجموعات الآثار المصرية فيها. وكان لهذه الجولة الأمريكية

نتائج مباشرة على المتحف الملكي للفن والتاريخ. فقد وصلت إلى بروكسل في عام 1928 هبةٌ كبيرة من الصور من متحف متروبوليتان للفنون بنيويورك، بما فيها أكثر من مائتي صورة للقطع الأثرية المنتمية إلى مجموعة اللورد كارنارفون (كابارت 10 :1982b). وفي عام 1932، عُيّن كابارت أمينًا استشاريًا لدى متحف بروكلين، مسؤولًا عن تطوير مجموعته المصرية؛ فانقسم وقتُه بين بروكسل وبروكلين حتى اندلاع الحرب العالمية الثانية. وخلال تلك السنوات، جرى إمداد مجموعة بروكسل بصور القطع الأثرية الموجودة في متحف بروكلين وفي مؤسسات أمريكية أخرى، من مثل متحف الفنون الجميلة في بوسطن وجمعية نيويورك التاريخية.

وبالنظر إلى هذه الإسهامات الدولية، ليس من المستغرب أن تضمَّ المجموعة الكاملة للمتحف الملكي اليوم نحو 3200 صورة سلبية زجاجية تغطي القطع الأثرية المصرية الموجودة في ثلاث قارات.

النبات والحيوان

ثمة مجموعة فرعية صغيرة ولكنها مهمة من أرشيف الصور الفوتوغرافية تضم صورًا التقطها عالم المصريات الألماني لودفيج (لويس) كيمر في أواخر العشرينات وأوائل الثلاثينيات من القرن العشرين (لينرت 2023). وكان كيمر قد غادر ألمانيا بعد وفاة معلمه جورج شفاينفورث عام 1925، وتوجّه إلى مصر، وانصبّ اهتمامُه على ما فيها من النباتات والحيوانات، مما شحذ همّة كابارت. وتم الاتفاق على أن يزوّد كيمر المتحف الملكي للفن والتاريخ بوثائق فوتوغرافية عن التراث النباتي والحيواني في مصر مقابل بدل سنوي. وبالتالي حصل كيمر على وسائل إضافية لمتابعة أبحاثه، وتمكّن كابارت من تطوير وإثراء أرشيف الصور الفوتوغرافية بموضوع جديد لم يكن قد حظي باهتمام كبير في السابق في أوساط علم المصريات. واستمر هذا التعاقد لمدة ثلاث سنوات من عام 1929 حتى عام 1932، ونشر كيمر عدة مقالات في مجلة «وقائع مصرية»[11]، وكان في ذلك الحين مهتمًا على وجه الخصوص بشجرة الحماط (تين فرعون)، وأعدَّ دراسة عنها لم تُنشر (الشكل 3). كما قام برحلة دراسة إلى الدلتا لاستكشاف زهرة اللوتس (باللاتينية Nelumbium speciosum، الشكل 4). وبالإضافة إلى الصور الفوتوغرافية، عمل على جمع القطع الأثرية الصغيرة والأشياء التي تُمثّل الحيوانات والنباتات، وباعها إلى المتحف الملكي.

الأهمية المادية الذاتية للصور الفوتوغرافية

تتضمن مجموعة الصور السلبية الزجاجية الموجودة في مكتبة الآثار المصرية بالمتحف الملكي للفن والتاريخ أكثر من 14 ألف عنصرًا، يعود أقدمُها إلى عام 1901 عندما قام جان كابارت بأول رحلة له إلى مصر، ويعود أحدثُها إلى حفريات عام 1955 في الكاب تحت إشراف بيير جيلبرت (1904-1986). ومن وجهة النظر الفنية، فإن غالبية الصور السلبية الزجاجية هي عبارة عن ألواح ومونوغرامات عادية. وقد التُقط ربع الصور تقريبًا بكاميرا بيليني مزدوجة العدسات (انظر أدناه) على ألواح زجاجية من مقاس 9 × 8 سم، منها 3200 صورة على الأقل تشكل 1600 صورة مزدوجة (الشكل 5).

لقد تَمثّلت إحدى الغايات من هذه المجموعة في تيسير استخدام الصور كوسائل توضيحية في المُحاضرات والفصول الدراسية. ولهذا جرى استنساخُها في شرائح ضوئية إيجابية زجاجية، خُزّنت أيضًا بالمتحف في خزانات خشبية (الشكل 6). وأضيفت على الشرائح الضوئية بطاقاتٌ مكتوبة بخط اليد تتضمن رقم كل صورة ووصف موجز لها (الشكل 7). في الوقت نفسه، احتُفظ بفهرس في مصنفَين من بطاقات الفهرسة الورقية المرتبة بحسب رقم الجرد أو الموقع الجغرافي. غير أن المعلومات الموجودة على بطاقات الفهرسة القديمة كانت جزئية للغاية وغير موحَّدة. لذلك، وضمن إطار مشروع «صورة»، جرى البحث عن بيانات وصفية جديدة لإضافتها إلى كل صورة. وكانت هذه الشرائح الضوئية قد ترحّلت بترحال كابارت لإلقاء المحاضرات على عامة الناس والطلاب وأمام مختلف المؤتمرات العلمية.

وفي عام 1928، وصف كابارت تفاصيل التقدم المحرز في مجموعة الصور الفوتوغرافية وكيفية إدارتها. ويوضح هذا الوصف أن المجموعة تكوّنت من الصور التي التقطها ومعاونوه خلال رحلاتهم، وكذلك من الشرائح الضوئية الزجاجية المنتجة تجاريًا والمشتراة من المتاحف في جميع أنحاء العالم ومن محلات التصوير الفوتوغرافي مثل محل سيف وقديس في الأقصر.

---

10. تقرير الرحلة الذي كتبه كابارت إلى أوجين فان أوفرلوب، 1907/8/4، أرشيف المتحف الملكي للفن والتاريخ، 31/61: تقرير الرحلة إلى إنجلترا 1907.

11. على سبيل المثال: كريمر 1931.

تعكس هذه الصور أيضًا شبكةَ كابارت المهنية الواسعة. ثمة المئات من الصور التي التقطها كابارت و/أو معاونيه عن مجريات الحفريات التي نظّمها قطاع الآثار المصرية والمؤسسات الأخرى من الجامعات والمتاحف والجمعيات العلمية. وفي النظرة العامة الواردة أدناه، لم تُذكر سوى الحفريات المشمولة في هذا الكتاب، من دون سرد كافة مشاريع العمل الميداني المدرجة في المجموعة الكاملة.

نظرة عامة على رحلات كابارت ومعاونيه إلى مصر

— ديسمبر 1900 - فبراير 1901: الزيارة الأولى

زار كابارت مصر للمرة الأولى في سن الثالثة والعشرين خلال شتاء 1900-1901. ولم يُحفَظ سوى عدد قليل جدًّا من صور تلك الرحلة في مجموعة الصور السلبية الزجاجية: إذ جرى تحديد عشر منها فقط. ومع ذلك، لا بد أنه أنتج الكثير من الصور في رحلته الأولى، من حيث إنه نشر عددًا منها في مقال له عن تجاربه وملاحظاته (كابارت 1901). وقد ركز اهتمامَه على المنطقتين الرئيسيتين في البلاد: شمالًا، القاهرة والمناطق المحيطة بها من أجل استيضاح معالم مدينة ممفيس (منف) القديمة؛ وجنوباً، الأقصر لاستبانة مدينة طيبة القديمة. وفي الكرنك، اطلع على الحفريات التي كان يجريها عالم المصريات الفرنسي جورج ليجرين لصالح قطاع الآثار المصرية.

— نوفمبر 1905 - يناير 1906: البعثة في مصطبة نفرتنف

كانت رحلة كابارت الثانية إلى مصر بمثابة بعثة استكشافية فعلية، بهدف البحث عن معبد في إحدى المصاطب الجنائزية العائدة إلى عصر الدولة القديمة لصالح المتحف الملكي للفن والتاريخ. وبعد عدة محاولات برفقة الآثاري البريطاني جيمس كويبل، استقر خياره على مصطبة «نفرتنف» وهو أحد كبار المسؤولين من الأسرة الخامسة والمدفون في سقارة في ظل هرم زوسر المدرّج (بروفيرتس 2005؛ جريزر أوهارا وآخرون 2023). فجرى تفكيك المعبد الجنائزي وإرسال كتل أحجاره الجيرية في صناديق فردية إلى بروكسل حيث أعيد بناؤه في المتحف في ربيع 1906. وخلال هذه الرحلة، زار كابارت العديد من المواقع الأخرى، بما فيها حفريات إدوارد نافيل في الدير البحري (لصالح صندوق استكشاف مصر). وقد وُثِّقت عملية تفكيك وإرسال المعبد بأكمله، بالإضافة إلى بقية الرحلة، في أكثر من 170 صورة سلبية زجاجية.

— فبراير - مارس 1907: هليوبوليس

بدعوة من الصناعي البلجيكي البارون إدوارد إمبان، نظّم كابارت أول بعثة أثرية له إلى مصر عام 1907 في رمال الصحراء العباسية إلى الشمال الشرقي من القاهرة (فان لو وبروير 2010؛ بروير ودويان 2019). وانضم إليه تلميذه تشارلز مائيان والبروفيسور فرناند ماينس من جامعة لوفان الكاثوليكية. فانكبوا على سبر الأراضي التي لا زالت بكرًا في ذلك الحين، بحثًا عن البقايا الأثرية، قبل أن يشرع إمبان ببناء مدينته الجديدة هليوبوليس. ولكنهم لم يعثروا على أية آثار قديمة في المنطقة، فوصف كابارت نفسه «بالصياد الفاشل». ووُثِّقت هذه البعثة في ما يقرب من مائتي صورة.

— مارس - أبريل 1909: أبيدوس

تمثّل الغرض من رحلة عام 1909 في تصوير معبد سيتي الأول الجنائزي في أبيدوس. وقد نشر كابارت دراسة مخصصة له في عام 1912 (كابارت 1912). وبدعوة من عالم المصريات البريطاني جون جارستانج من جامعة ليفربول الذي كان يعمل هناك في ذلك الوقت، مكث عشرة أيام في دار التنقيب التابعة له في الصحراء، مما أتاح له تمضية وقت طويل في المعبد. وفي المجمل، ثمة نحو 140 صورة لهذه الرحلة في الأرشيف.

— فبراير - مارس 1923: توت عنخ آمون مع الملكة إليزابيث

على إثر اكتشاف مقبرة توت عنخ آمون في نوفمبر 1922، قررت إليزابيث ملكة بلجيكا أن تكون حاضرة عند فتح حُجرة الدفن في فبراير 1923 (كابارت 1923؛ بروفيرتس 1998). فسافرت إلى مصر مع ابنها ولي العهد الأمير ليوبولد برفقة جان كابارت كمرشد لها. وفي أعقاب الزيارة، شرع الزوار في رحلة نهرية عبر النيل وتوقفوا في العديد من المواقع. ثمة 116 صورة موجودة في الأرشيف لهذه الرحلة، تُكملها المحفوظات الفوتوغرافية الأخرى، لا سيما تلك الموجودة في القصر الملكي ببروكسل حيث يُحتفَظ بألبومات صور الملكة الشخصية.

— أبريل 1925: رحلة دراسية مع الطلاب

عام 1925، مثّل كابارت بلجيكا في المؤتمر الجغرافي الدولي الحادي عشر الذي انعقد في القاهرة في الفترة ما بين الأول والتاسع من أبريل، والذي كان أول مؤتمر من نوعه بعد الحرب العالمية الأولى. واصطحب معه ابنته الكبرى إليزابيث إلى جانب العديد من طلابه: إليونور بيل-دي موت، ماري فينانتس-روندي، ديزي جولدشميت، دينيز فابيس. وانضم إلى المجموعة مارسيلا فيربروك وبودوان فان دي فال في القاهرة. فقاموا معًا بزيارة المواقع والمتاحف في الإسكندرية والقاهرة ومصر الوسطى ومنطقة الأقصر. وأضيفت أكثر من 200 صورة سلبية زجاجية لهذه الرحلة إلى المجموعة.

— يناير - مارس 1927: تل هو

من 14 وحتى 20 فبراير، أجرى فريق مؤسسة الملكة إليزابيث لعلم المصريات حملة أثرية في تل هو بصعيد مصر (كابارت 1927). وبرفقة عدد من معاونيه، كانت تلك أول رحلة إلى مصر قامت بها زوجة كابارت مارجريت ثيرونيت التي تَظهر في العديد من الصور التي يصل عددها إلى نحو مائتي صورة محفوظة في الأرشيف.

— يناير - مارس 1929: البعثة الفوتوغرافية

في عام 1929، سافر جان كابارت إلى مصر لأداء مهمة محدّدة واحدة وهي تصوير القطع الأثرية في المتحف المصري بالقاهرة، والآثار والمواقع في منطقة ممفيس (منف) التي لم تكن ممثلة تمثيلًا كافيًا في الأرشيفات الفوتوغرافية (كابارت 1929). وذهب إلى صعيد مصر حيث زار مواقع الحفريات الأثرية التي كان يقودها زملاؤه الفرنسيون والأمريكيون. ومن هذه الرحلة احتُفظ بما يقرب من مائة لوح زجاجي.

— يناير - إبريل 1930: رحلة عائلة جولدمان والرحلة الملكية

في الثاني من مارس، عادت بنا الباخرة «الفسطاط» الميمونة إلى القاهرة، وفي جعبتنا الكثير من الصور والعديد من القطع الأثرية المقتناة على طول الطريق.
(كابارت 1930a: 188)

تعود الغالبية العظمى من الصور السلبية الزجاجية في المجموعة إلى رحلة عام 1930. ولا عجب من ذلك، لأن كابارت قام في ذلك العام برحلتين متتاليتين عبر مصر من الشمال إلى الجنوب (بروفيرتس 2006). الأولى كانت عبارة عن رحلة نهرية في النيل مع عائلة جولدمان الأمريكية على متن الباخرة «الفسطاط» التابعة لشركة توماس كوك (انظر الصورة رقم 190)، وذلك من يناير حتى أوائل مارس (كابارت 1930a). ومن بعدها مباشرةً، انضم إلى زيارة الدولة التي قام بها ملك بلجيكا ألبرت الأول وحرمه الملكة إليزابيث لمصر، ورافق الملكة في رحلتها عبر النيل بعد مغادرة الملك إلى بغداد بالطائرة (كابارت 1930b) (الشكل 2). وقد وُثِّقت رحلة عائلة جولدمان في ما يقارب 250 صورة، في حين تُقطت نحو مائة صورة للزيارة الملكية الثانية. كما زار كابارت عددًا من مواقع التنقيب، بما فيها حفريات روبرت موند في أرمنت (لصالح جمعية استكشاف مصر).

— ديسمبر 1933 - فبراير 1934: العمارنة

بصفته أمينًا استشاريًا لمتحف بروكلين، استطاع كابارت إقناع المتحف بالمساهمة في تمويل بعثة جمعية استكشاف مصر في العمارنة تحت إشراف جون بيندلبري. في يناير 1934، سافر كابارت إلى هناك مع زوجته مارجريت وعدد من مساعديه (كابارت وفيربروك 1934)، ومكث قرابة أسبوعين في دار التنقيب البريطانية، وقام بتوثيق الأعمال الأثرية وتنظيم الرحلات الاستكشافية إلى مختلف المواقع في مصر. فزار على سبيل المثال البعثات الفرنسية في تانيس (صان الحجر) بالدلتا (تحت إشراف بيير مونتيه)، وفي الطود بصعيد مصر (تحت إشراف فرناند بيسون دي لا روك). ويحتفظ الأرشيف من هذه الرحلة بأكثر من 325 صورة سلبية.

— فبراير - مارس 1937: البعثة الأولى في الكاب

دامت بعثة الكاب الأولى من فبراير إلى مارس 1937، بقيادة جان كابارت ومجموعة صغيرة من معاونيه: مارسيلا فيربروك، أرباج مختياريان، إليونور بيل-دي موت، فيوليت فيرهوجن. كما انضم المهندس المعماري جان ستينون إلى الفريق بناءً على توصية فيكتور هورتا رائد الفن الجديد «الآرت نوفو». وكان رئيس العمال المصريين شارد محمد منصور. وخلال الموسم الأول من العمل الميداني، ركز الفريق البلجيكي جهوده على معبدَي نخبت وتحوت ضمن الأسوار العالية[9]. ويحتوي الأرشيف على ما يقرب من 150 صورة عن هذا الموسم.

---

9. للحصول على نظرة عامة على الأعمال الميدانية البلجيكية في الكاب، انظر ليم 2008. يلخص كتاب نشره كابارت في أعقاب موسم 1945-1946 العملَ والحياة في الكاب خلال حملات التنقيب الثلاث (كابارت 1946).

وبعد الانتهاء من هذه الخطوة، وُضعت خطةُ حفظ طويلة الأمد واتُّخذت تدابير محددة للصون، بما في ذلك إعادة تغليف الألواح الزجاجية في أظرف فردية ضمن علب خالية من الأحماض. ولتجنب تعرّضها للمزيد من الضرر النهائي، خُزِّنت الآن في بيئة توفر الحماية وذات مناخ خاضع للتحكم.

تمثّل الهدف الرئيسي لمشروع «صورة» في فهرسة الصور الرقمية ضمن النظام المركزي لإدارة المجموعات[15] في المتحف الملكي للفن والتاريخ، جنبًا إلى جنب مع البيانات الوصفية الجديدة. وفضلًا عن المعلومات الفنية لكل صورة (المقاسات، نوع الصورة، حالة الحفظ)، تَوجّب وضعُ وصفٍ لمضامينها. وبهذا كانت الخطوة الثانية بمثابة المراجعة النقدية للبيانات (الوصفية) المتاحة لكل صورة فردية، والتي تألفت من العبارات المكتوبة بخط اليد على اللوحة الزجاجية (الإيجابية) والبطاقات الورقية في فهرسين. ولم تتضمّن بطاقات الفهرسة إلا معلومات محدودة للغاية، مثل المكان والتاريخ واسم المصور. وكانت المعلومات التفصيلية عن الآثار وأجزائها وتوجّهها وأسماء الأشخاص الذين يظهرون في الصور، غير متوفرة. وحتى المعلوماتِ الأساسيةَ عن إطار التصوير (المصور، التاريخ) لم تُسجَّل دومًا. فقام فريق مشروع «صورة» باستكمال البيانات الوصفية المتاحة بأكبر قدر ممكن من المعلومات الإضافية. ولهذا الغرض، أثبتت أرشيفات المتحف أنها منجم ذهب فعلي، من حيث احتوائها على مصادر قيّمة، كدفاتر كابارت الشخصية ويومياته ورسائله إلخ. وفي مرحلة لاحقة، سوف يجري توفير هذه المراجع على شكل روابط متقاطعة مع مكتبة المتحف على الإنترنت وكتالوج أرشيفه، بما في ذلك الوصول إلى النسخ الإلكترونية من المنشورات والمواد الأرشيفية عند الإمكان.

وسيتم أيضًا ربط صور القطع الأثرية المخزّنة في المتحف بالقطع الأثرية الواردة في كتالوج المتحف على الإنترنت. وفي المستقبل، سيجري توسيع هذا الربط، عند الاقتضاء، ليشمل كتالوجات المتاحف الأخرى على الإنترنت، وبالتالي إعادة إنشاء شبكة كابارت الدولية في العالم الرقمي.

ويطمح المشروع إلى ما هو أبعد من مجرّد إتاحة هذه الصور عبر الإنترنت. فقد عنصرًا البحث في الأرشيف وقاعدة البيانات على سبيل المثال، بالتوصل إلى رؤى جديدة بشأن المصطبة رقم RMAH E.02465، وكشف معلومات جديدة عن موقعها الأصلي في سقارة، وعن جميع المصاطب التي رفضها كابارت قبل اختياره لهذه (جريزر أوهارا وآخرون 2023). وثمة مسار بحثي آخر مهتم بالعمال المصريين (أهالي قفط والعمال المحليين من منطقة الكاب)، الذين عملوا مع فريق كابارت في الكاب ويظهرون في العديد من الصور (دي ماير وآخرون 2023b).

مختارات من الصور

كان كابارت يعلّق أهمية كبيرة على حجّية كلماته، ولكنه فهم أكثر من أي شخص آخر، قوةَ الصور والحاجة إلى توضيح محاضراته بأفضل الصور الممكنة، واختارها بعناية شديدة، ولم يرض قط بأية صورة من نوعية متوسطة أو رديئة.

(دي كايزر 1947:210)

رأى كابارت أن التوثيقَ البصري لا يقل أهمية عن التوثيق المكتوب، وقد جمع بين الاثنين بطريقة قد تبدو بديهية في عالم اليوم المشبع بالصور، ولكنها لم تكن متّبعة في النصف الأول من القرن العشرين. وعلى الرغم من أنه بطبيعة الحال لم يقرأ مقالات سوزان سونتاج «عن التصوير الفوتوغرافي» التي صدرت لاحقًا في السبعينيات من القرن العشرين، إلا أنه كان سيتّفق مع رؤيتها الواردة في السطور الافتتاحيّة لمقالها «كهف أفلاطون»، حيث كتبتْ:

في كهف أفلاطون، يلبث البشر مستمتعين بعاداتهم القديمة وبظلال الأشياء وخيالاتها بلا فائدة تُرجى. غير أن التعلّم من خلال الصور الفوتوغرافية يختلف عن التعلّم من الرسوم القديمة التي صنعتها يدُ الصانع. وذلك لسبب واحد هو أن في متناولنا كمًّا هائلًا من الصور التي تسترعي انتباهَنا. فقد انطلق التصوير الفوتوغرافي في عام 1839، ومنذ ذلك الحين جرى تصوير كل شيء تقريبًا. ومن شأن هذا النهم الشديد للتصوير أن يغير ظروف الحبس في الكهف، أي في العالم الذي نعيش فيه. لأن الصور الفوتوغرافية تعلّمنا قانونًا بصريًا جديدًا وتغيّر وتوسّع مفاهيمَنا عمّا يستحق النظر إليه وما يحقّ لنا مراقبتَه. وتشكل الصور قواعدَ نحوية جديدة، وأخلاقياتٍ جديدةً للرؤية. وأخيرًا، تمثّل أعظمُ نتيجة حققتها مغامرةُ التصوير الفوتوغرافي، في إعطائنا الإحساس بالاحتفاظ بالعالم كله في أذهاننا من خلال مختارات من الصور.

(سونتاج 1970:3)

استُنسخت في هذا الكتاب 202 صورة لا تشكّل سوى مجموعة صغيرة من الأرشيف الضخم الموصوف أعلاه. وقد حاول فريق مؤسسة الملكة إليزابيث لعلم المصريات من خلالها الاحتفاظ بعالم مصر القديمة والحديثة في أذهانهم. واختيرت هذه الصور بناءً على اعتبارات موضوعية وجمالية. علمًا أن خيار رقمنتها ودراستها في هذا الوقت ليس عشوائيًا، من حيث إنه يتزامن مع مبادرات أخرى تبحث في تطور علم المصريات في السياق البلجيكي وعلاقاته الوثيقة مع الأسرة الملكية والصناعة في النصف الأول من القرن العشرين. ومن بين هذه المبادرات مشروع «الأهرامات والتقدم: النزعة التوسعية البلجيكية وعلم المصريات، 1830-1952» (دي ماير وآخرون 2019)، وهو مشروع متعدد التخصصات يجمع المؤرخين المعاصرين وعلماء المصريات وأمناء الأرشيفات من خمس مؤسسات جامعية ومتحفية بلجيكية، وكان من بين إنجازاته إصدارُ سيرة حياة جان كابارت (برفيرت 2022)، مرفقةً بصور من أرشيف الألواح الزجاجية الخاضعة للدراسة ضمن مشروع «صورة». وفي الفترة من مارس إلى أكتوبر 2023، سوف يحتضن المتحف الملكي للفن والتاريخ معرضًا واسعًا بعنوان «البعثة إلى مصر»، سيتناول تطور علم المصريات في بلجيكا من القرن التاسع عشر وحتى اليوم، وسَتُعرض فيه صورٌ من مجموعة المتحف. هذه مجرد أمثلة قليلة على الجهود المتضافرة التي تبذلها بلجيكا دولة للتحقيق النقدي في نشأة هذا الفرع العلمي، من دون أن تتحاشى مواجهة ماضيها الاستعماري (فانهول 2023).

بنية الكتاب

إن التصنيف المنتظم للصور وفقًا للتسلسل الجغرافي أو لفئات لفتة الأفكار، سوف يسمح بمضاعفة قيمة الوثائق التي في حوزتنا.

(كابارت 1932:6)

لم يتحقّق تنظيم الصور وفق التسلسل الجغرافي الذي تصوّره كابارت في عام 1932 في حياته. وحتى اليوم، لا تزال الشرائح الضوئية مصنفة وفقًا للترتيب الذي كانت عليه قبل عقود. ولكن هذا الكتاب يعرض الصور بالتسلسل الجغرافي، بحيث يأخذ القارئ في رحلة عبر النيل على خطى كابارت ومعاونيه، انطلاقًا من نزولهم في ميناء الإسكندرية، وصولًا إلى موقع سمنة المحصن في السودان الحديث وأقصى نقطة أدركتها رحلاتهم في الجنوب. ويشار إلى جميع المواقع المذكورة في الكتاب على الخريطة الواردة في صفحة 23.

وقد أُرفقت كلُّ صورة بوصف موجز وبمعلومات عن المصور والتاريخ عند توفرها. وفي بعض الأحيان، سمحت يوميات كابارت ومراسلاته المحفوظة، بتحديد التاريخ الدقيق للصورة. وفي أحيان أخرى، كانت المعلومات الموجودة على بطاقة الفهرس الورقية الأصلية ضئيلة، ولم يُسفر البحث الأرشيفي نفسه سوى عن ربط الصورة بسنة معينة. وينطبق الشيء نفسه على تحديد هوية الأشخاص الظاهرين في الصور. وبفضل اليوميات والأرشيفات، تم التعرف ليس فقط على أقارب كابارت والمتعاونين معه، ولكن أيضًا على العديد من أصدقائه وزملائه المصريين.

ليست كل الأسماء والفترات والأماكن المذكورة في هذا الكتاب مألوفةً لغير المختصّين بالمصريات. ولذلك، وُضع مسرد في الصفحة 234، مع معلومات أساسية موجزة عن الأشخاص المذكورين، بالإضافة إلى تعريفات للكلمات المصرية (القديمة) والعربية المستخدمة. ويخدم هذا المسرد أيضًا كفهرس يشير إلى أرقام الصور في الكتاب. وثمة، في الصفحة 22، نظرة عامة على الفترات التاريخية المصرية وفقًا للتسلسل الزمني.

https://www.carmentis.be/eMP/eMuseumPlus .15

كما قلتُ سابقاً، تمثّلت الحصيلة الرئيسية لرحلاتنا في إثراء أرشيفات الصور الفوتوغرافية لدينا. فقبل بضع سنوات، كان لدينا نحو ألفي صورة كنتُ قد التقطتُ معظمَها خلال رحلاتي عبر مصر وفي متاحف أوروبا منذ عام 1899. ومن حينها أضفنا أكثر من ثلاثة آلاف صورة أخرى، بما في ذلك ألف صورة من سلسلة سيف وقدّيس الممتازة، وخمسمائة من الوثائق التي أحضرتُها الآنستان فيربروك وبود من طيبة. [...]

من برلين، أحضرنا أكثر من مائة صورة النُقط العديد منها خُصّيصاً للمؤسسة على يد الآنسة جرانتز التي تستحق الثناء على موهبتها ولطافتها. كما قدّم لنا هيلدسهايم وليدي عددًا من الوثائق الثمينة. ووعدنا لايبزيغ وهانوفر بتزويدنا بالصور. فضلاً عن ذلك سوف نبعث أحد المصورين المتحفيين لمتابعة برنامجنا مع مجموعة شيرلر في لاهاي.

أما نيويورك فقد أرسلت أكثر من مائتي صورة من مجموعة كارنارفون؛ وسوف أتلقى نحو أربعمائة صورة أخرى وفقًا للقوائم التي جمعتُها بعد تصفّحي للإلبومات الموجودة في غرفة الدراسة في قسم المصريات. ويتضمن برنامج بوسطن حوالي مائة صورة، بما في ذلك عدد من الصور لنقوش المصاطب التي سُلتقط خصّيصاً لصالحنا.

ونتوقع وصولَ صور من أكسفورد وكامبريدج وكوبنهاغن وهامبورغ. وقد حصلنا على كامل سلسلة الوثائق المصرية من المحفوظات الفوتوغرافية للفن والتاريخ بباريس.

فور وصول جميع هذه الصور إلى بروكسل، يجري ترقيمُها وتقييدها في السجلات، وتصنيفُها وفهرستها على البطاقات. وقد وَجدت الآنسة فيربروك من أجل هذا العمل المُضني، مساعِدةً ذكيةً مثلها في شخص الآنسة دي موت.

وفي الوقت ذاته، وقبل تصنيفها النهائي، تُرسل الصور الأكثر أهمية إلى أستوديو المتحف ليجري استنساخُها في شرائح ضوئية. وبهذا أضفنا ألف لوح ضوئي جديد إلى مجموعاتنا، فازدادت أهميتها يوماً بعد يوم في إعداد الدروس والمؤتمرات.

(كابارت 10- 9 :1928b)

وبهذا جرى تصوير العديد من الصور التي اشتراها كابارت أو حصل عليها مطبوعةً من زملائه، وحُوّلت إلى شرائح ضوئية. يعطي الشكل 8 مثالاً على طبع إحدى الصور الفوتوغرافية التي التقطها أنطونيو بياتو، في حين يبيّن الشكل 9 مثالاً على طبع مجموعة من الصور الجوية لمصر التقطها ثيودور كوفلر في عام 1914[12]. فضلاً عن ذلك، جرى تصوير الرسومات التوضيحية في المنشورات المصرية التي اعتُبرت ضرورية للمحاضرات. وفي العديد من الصور، يمكن رؤية المعدات غريبة الشكل المستخدمة لتيسير هذه العملية، بدءًا من دبابيس تثبيت الصور المطبوعة إلى الألواح الخشبية (الشكل 8 و9)، مرورًا بالمساطر المعدنية لتثبيت الحواف (الأشكال 10-12)، والحوامل المتقنة لتسهيل تصوير الصور المطبوعة الكبيرة (الشكل 13) وقوالب الجبس المنسوخة عن كِسر المنحوتات (الشكل 14).

وفي بعض الحالات النادرة، تعطي هذه الصور فكرة عن المنتجات المستخدمة في ذلك الوقت. ففي الشكل 15 على سبيل المثال نرى علبة للشرائح الضوئية من ماركة «هاوف» (12 شريحة من قياس 10 × 8.5) اشتُريت من دار جيسيل وأفانزو للعدسات الفوتوغرافية فرع بروكسل. ونرى في الشكل 16 أربع علب من الشرائح الضوئية الزجاجية من ماركات «أجفا» و جيفرت وجيمينو»، استُعملت لتثبيت صفحات أحد الكتب. أما في الشكل 17، فنلاحظ يدَين تمسكان كتابًا شُوّيت صفحاته بين لوح خشبي ولوح زجاجي، وأسند على علبة من الألواح الزجاجية الألمانية من شركة «ميموسا» في درسدن.

وقد تطلّب التعاملُ مع الألواح الزجاجية في المتحف ترتيبات لوجستية واسعة، فما بالك بالتعامل معها في الميدان بمصر، حيث لزم شراء الألواح الثقيلة من المتاجر المتخصصة ثم حملُها وتحميضُها محلّيًا (الشكل 18). لقد تطرّق كابارت على الدوام إلى هذه الترتيبات، كما هو الحال عندما كتب في يومياته في 12 فبراير 1930: «تلقّيت الصور الأول من لينرت: عشرين علبة بنتائج جيدة جدًّا على العموم. لا أعرف ماذا أفعل مع اللمعان والانعكاسات التي لا تزال تَظهر في بعض الألواح. سوف أرسل الصور السلبية والمطبوعة إلى بروكسل لتسهيل عملية التصنيف». وخلال الرحلة الطويلة على النيل مع عائلة جولدمان، نَفَذَت

الألواحُ الزجاجية لديه في أسوان. فكتب في 23 فبراير 1930: «استفدتُ من وقت الاستراحة للذهاب والتقاط صورتين مجسمتين (ستريوسكوب) للمسلة في المحجر. هذه هي آخر الألواح الزجاجية في جعبتي. والطلبية التي أمرت بإرسالها لم تصل بعد». وبعد ثلاثة أيام: «لم يردني حتى اليوم أيُّ خبر عن الألواح». وفي 3 مارس، كتب: «سآخذ الألواح الفوتوغرافية النهائية إلى لينرت لتحميضها». والأستوديو الذي أشار إليه مرتين هو أستوديو لينرت ولاندروك، أحد أقدم محلات التصوير الفوتوغرافي في القاهرة، ولا يزال قائمًا حتى اليوم.[13]

كابارت وكاميرته بيليني مزدوجة العدسات

كانت الكاميرا التي حملها كابارت معه أينما ذهب في مصر من نوع بيليني مزدوجة العدسات (ستريو). وغالبًا ما أتى على ذكرها بنفسه. وقد أشارت مارسيلا فيربروك في نعيها له إلى مدى الترابط الوثيق بين الاثنين:

تحتفظ المؤسسة من كل منهما كشهادة صادقة وبليغة، بكاميرا بيليني رفيقته التي لازمته على الدوام. فأستاذُنا في علم المصريات كان أيضًا أستاذُنا في التصوير الفوتوغرافي، وقد استطاع أن يلتقط بصوره روحَ مصر.

(فيربروك، 1947: 194)

يظهر كابارت في الشكل 19 وهو يلتقط صورة بكاميرا بيليني هذه في صحراء أبيدوس في عام 1930، ونراه في الصورة رقم 145 وهو يستخدمها في مدينة هابو في العام نفسه. ويحتفظ المتحف الملكي للفن والتاريخ بالحقيبة التي استخدمها لحمل لوحاته الزجاجية (الشكل 20)، غير أن الكاميرا كانت قد اختفت منذ فترة طويلة. لكنها عادت إلى الظهور مؤخرًا بفضل قوة وسائل الإعلام. ففي أعقاب عرض مشروع «صورة» على قناة RTBF الإخبارية بتاريخ 27 يناير 2021، حيث ذُكر أن كاميرا كابارت قد ضاعت، اتصلت بنا السيدة آنلي كاميون من بروكسل قائلةً إن الكاميرا في حوزتها (الشكل 21)، حيث إنها مع زوجها يديران متجرًا للكاميرات ويجمعان الكاميرات القديمة والكلاسيكية. ومنذ عدة أعوام، أهداها زوجُها كاميرا كابارت التي باعها له أحدُ أحفاده. وإلى جانب التاريخ الموثّق الذي يؤكد أصالة الكاميرا، ثمة لوحة عاجية صغيرة مثبّتة عليها وقد نُقشت عليها العبارة التالية: «الدكتور كابارت، 5 شارع إجمونت، بروكسل»، في إثبات على أن الكاميرا كانت في الأصل لوالد جان ألفونس كابارت، الطبيب جان ألفونس كابارت.

مشروع «صورة»

على مدى النصف الأول من القرن العشرين، حظيت مجموعة الصور الفوتوغرافية في المتحف الملكي للفن والتاريخ بالاعتراف الدولي، ولكن أوساط المصريات في وقت لاحق لم تعد تعلم بمحتواها، ولا حتى بوجودها. وأدّى غياب الاهتمام بها إلى إهمالها على الرغم من قيمتها التاريخية العظيمة، وطوى النسيانُ صورَ السنوات الرائدة في علم المصريات البلجيكي ومهارات كابارت الفوتوغرافية. ويرجع هذا جزئيًا إلى تعذّر الوصول إلى المجموعة وعدم وجود قاعدة بيانات قابلة للبحث بشأنها. ولمعالجة هذا القصور، أُطلق مشروع «صورة»[14] في عام 2020 بالتعاون بين المتحف الملكي وعلماء المصريات في جامعة لوفن الكاثوليكية (جريزر أوهارا وآخرون 2021؛ فان دير بيرغ وآخرون 2021). وتماشياً مع طموح كابارت الأصلي، يهدف مشروع «صورة» لدراسة هذه المجموعة ومشاركتها رقميًا مع الأوساط العلمية الدولية وعامة الناس على حدٍّ سواء.

وقد أدى تضافر شروط التخزين غير المناسبة والإهمال الذي دام لعقود طويلة، إلى ظهور آثار تدهور كيميائي وبيولوجي على بعض الألواح الزجاجية، مما تطلّب اتخاذَ إجراءات فورية من أجل حفظ هذه المجموعة للإجيال القادمة. وكخطوة أولى، تمت رقمنة المجموعة بأكملها بدقة عالية في المرصد الملكي البلجيكي، باستخدام أحدث التقنيات التي جرى تطويرها في الأصل لرقمنة ألواح التصوير الفلكي؛ فقد اقتضت رقمنة صور النجوم الزجاجية إنشاء مجموعة بيانات رقمية عالية الدقة. وقد سمح استخدام هذه التسهيلات مع مجموعة صور المتحف بإنشاء صور رقمية عالية الجودة ومفصّلة بشكل يكاد لا يُصدّق.

---

12. للمزيد من المعلومات عن الصور الجوية التي التقطها كوفلر، انظر بياشتيني 2014 و2015.
13. للاطلاع على تاريخ موجز للينرت ولاندروك، انظر https://egyptswiss.wixsite.com/yehia/lehnert-and-landrock (الدخول في 19/12/2022).
14. www.sura-project.be (الدخول في 19/12/2022).

التسميات التوضيحية للإشكال الواردة في المقدمة

الشكل 1. فريق مؤسسة الملكة إليزابيث لعلم المصريات نحو عام 1930. وقوفًا (من اليسار إلى اليمين): مارسيل هومبرت، أرباج مختاريان، جان كابارت، سيرجي مياسنيكوف. جلوسًا (من اليسار إلى اليمين): كلير بريو، مارسيلا فيربروك، سوزان بيرجيه (الحقوق محفوظة – المتحف الملكي للفن والتاريخ، رقم الجرد EGI-2.24397)

الشكل 2. إليزابيث ملكة بلجيكا وجان كابارت في محاجر الجرانيت في أسوان، بتصوير بول بولينيت في 29 مارس 1930 (الحقوق محفوظة – المتحف الملكي للفن والتاريخ، رقم الجرد EGI.07557)

الشكل A.3. غصن من شجر الحماط (تين فرعون Ficus sycomorus) مع ثمار التين من جزيرة الروضة، بتصوير لودفيج (لويس) كيمر في 7 يونيو 1929 (الحقوق محفوظة – المتحف الملكي للفن والتاريخ، رقم الجرد EGI.07794)؛ B. لودفيج (لويس) كيمر على شجرة الحماط، تاريخ الصورة 7 يونيو 1929 (الحقوق محفوظة – المتحف الملكي للفن والتاريخ، رقم الجرد EGI-2.07970)

الشكل A.4. برعم اللوتس (Nelumbium speciosum) منتصبًا في وسط البركة (الحقوق محفوظة – المتحف الملكي للفن والتاريخ، رقم الجرد EGI.07827)؛ B. زهرة اللوتس (الحقوق محفوظة – المتحف الملكي للفن والتاريخ، رقم الجرد EGI.07829)

الشكل 5. صورة مزدوجة مجسمة (ستيريو) لبوابة شيشنق الثالث في معبد آمون بصان الحجر (تانيس)، بتصوير جان كابارت عام 1934 (الحقوق محفوظة – المتحف الملكي للفن والتاريخ، رقم الجرد EGI.10025)

الشكل 6. الخزائن الخشبية التي تُحفظ فيها الشرائح الضوئية الزجاجية في مكتبة علم المصريات بالمتحف الملكي للفن والتاريخ. A. نحو عام 1930 (الحقوق محفوظة – المتحف الملكي للفن والتاريخ، رقم الجرد EGI-2.21543، مصور مجهول)؛ B. في يومنا هذا (بتصوير م. دي ماير)؛ C. صورة تفصيلية للإدراج (بتصوير ف. كلايس)

الشكل 7. شرائح ضوئية زجاجية وبطاقاتها التعريفية. A. داخل درج الخزانة (بتصوير م. دي ماير)؛ B. مختارات من الشرائح الضوئية (الحقوق محفوظة – المتحف الملكي للفن والتاريخ)

الشكل 8. صورة مطبوعة التقطها أنطونيو بياتو لتمثال أمنحتب الثالث في معبد الأقصر والذي غُدّل في عهد رمسيس الثاني لتمثيله (الحقوق محفوظة – المتحف الملكي للفن والتاريخ، رقم الجرد EGI.02471)

الشكل 9. صورة جوية لمعبد الأقصر بتصوير ثيودور كوفلر عام 1914 (الحقوق محفوظة – المتحف الملكي للفن والتاريخ، رقم الجرد EGI.00097)

الشكل 10. العمال في الكاب بتصوير جان ستينون عام 1937. صورتان مرتبطتان معاً على لوح خشبي أُعيد تصويرهما للتوصل إلى صورة أفقية (الحقوق محفوظة – المتحف الملكي للفن والتاريخ، رقم الجرد EGI.11411)

الشكل 11. جان كابارت على قاعدة تمثال ضخم لأمنحتب الثالث الضخم أو حورمحب في معبد الكرنك، بتصوير الملكة إليزابيث عام 1923 (الحقوق محفوظة – المتحف الملكي للفن والتاريخ، رقم الجرد EGI.02994)

الشكل 12. مجموعة من تماثيل القطط من الشيخ عبادة/أنتينوبوليس ضمن مجموعة المتحف الملكي للفن والتاريخ (الحقوق محفوظة – المتحف الملكي للفن والتاريخ، رقم الجرد .Inv EGI.05713)

الشكل 13. صورة للصحيفة 11 المنشورة في كالفرلي، آميس وبروم، ميرتل ف. 1935. The Temple of King Sethos I at Abydos, Volume II: The Chapels of Amen-Re', Re'-Harakhti, Ptah and King Sethos لندن: جمعية استكشاف مصر. شيكاغو: المعهد الشرقي في جامعة شيكاغو، 1935. يظهر في هذا الرسم بيد آميس كالفرلي الملك سيتي الأول وهو يقدّم القرابين إلى القوارب المقدسة للآلهة آمون رع وموت وخونسو؛ مصور مجهول، بعد عام 1935 (الحقوق محفوظة – المتحف الملكي للفن والتاريخ، رقم الجرد EGI.01552)

الشكل 14. صورة لقالب جبسي عن منحوتة من عصر الدولة الحديثة محفوظ في متحف اللوفر بباريس؛ المصور والتاريخ مجهولان (الحقوق محفوظة – المتحف الملكي للفن والتاريخ، رقم الجرد EGI.02828)

الشكل 15. صورة للصحيفة 8 المنشورة في كويبل، جيمس إدوارد 1913. Excavations at Saqqara (1911–12): The Tomb of Hesy. القاهرة: قطاع الآثار المصرية. المجلد مسنود على علبة للشرائح الضوئية من ماركة «هاوف»؛ مصور مجهول، بعد عام 1913 (الحقوق محفوظة – المتحف الملكي للفن والتاريخ، رقم الجرد EGI.02607)

الشكل 16. صورة للصحيفة 88 المنشورة في كاساس، لويس فرانسوا 1799. Voyage pittoresque de la Syrie, de la Phénicie, de la Palestine et de la Basse-Egypte باريس: بدون اسم. يظهر في الرسم قبر دهن المنحوت بالصخر من عصر الدولة القديمة في جبانة محجر خفرع بالجيزة. استُخدمت أربع علب للشرائح الضوئية (من ماركات «أجفا، جيفرت وجيمينو») لتثبيت الصفحات؛ مصور مجهول (الحقوق محفوظة – المتحف الملكي للفن والتاريخ، رقم الجرد EGI.04270)

الشكل 17. صورة للصحيفة 4 المنشورة في لوير، جان-فيليب 1936. La pyramide à degrés 1 : l'architecture. القاهرة: مطبعة المعهد الفرنسي للآثار الشرقية. تُظهر الصورة رسماً يعيد تشكيل مجمع هرم زوسر المدرج في سقارة؛ مصور مجهول، بعد عام 1936 (الحقوق محفوظة – المتحف الملكي للفن والتاريخ، رقم الجرد EGI.11012)

الشكل 18. رسالة من ع. قديس و ج. سيف (محل للصور في الأقصر) تُصادق على طلبية من طرف كابارت لطباعة الصور، 28 أكتوبر 1921 (الحقوق محفوظة – المتحف الملكي للفن والتاريخ)

الشكل 19. كابارت وهو يلتقط صورة بكاميرته بيليني في صحراء أبيدوس؛ لقطة مثبّتة من فيلم صوّره يوليوس جولدمان عام 1930 (الحقوق محفوظة – ثيودور ليهمان، بإذن من جامعة هارفارد)

الشكل 20. حقيبة لحمل الألواح الفوتوغرافية الزجاجية، محفوظة في المتحف الملكي للفن والتاريخ (بتصوير م. دي ماير)

الشكل 21. كاميرا كابارت مزدوجة العدسات بيليني بحوزة الآنسة آنلي كامبيون (بتصوير م. دي ماير)

رامانت-بيترز، أنيس. 1994
Rammant-Peeters, Agnes (ed.). 1994. *Palmen en tempels: Fotografie in Egypte in de XIXᵉ eeuw / La photographie en Égypte au XIXᵉ siècle / 19th-century Photography in Egypt*. Leuven, Peeters.

سونتاج، سوزان. 1977
Sontag, Susan. 1977. *On Photography*. London, Penguin Books.

فان دير بير، أثينا؛ كلايس، فوتر؛ دي ماير، مارلين؛ جريزر أوهارا، أود. 2021
Van der Perre, Athena; Claes, Wouter; De Meyer, Marleen & Gräzer Ohara, Aude. 2021. 'Sura-project: Het ontstaan van de Belgische Egyptologie in beeld'. *Ta-Mery* 14: 88–111.

فان لو، آن؛ برووير، ماري-سيسيل. 2010
Van Loo, Anne & Bruwier, Marie-Cécile (eds) 2010. *Héliopolis*. Brussels, Fonds Mercator.

فانهول، دوريان. 2023
Vanhulle, Dorian. 2023. *Une ancienne collection royale aux Musées royaux d'Art et d'Histoire de Bruxelles : Les antiquités égyptiennes du roi Léopold II* (Orientalia Lovaniensia Analecta). Leuven, Peeters.

فيربروك، مارسيلا. 1947
Werbrouck, Marcelle. 1947. 'Jean Capart et la Fondation Égyptologique Reine Élisabeth'. *Chronique d'Égypte* 22(44): 192–196.

فيربروك، مارسيلا. 1949
Werbrouck, Marcelle. 1949. 'Assemblée générale 8 octobre 1848 : Rapport de la directrice'. *Chronique d'Égypte* 24(47): 5–9.

ييلز، أنيسا. 2020
Yelles, Anissa. 2020. *Aux origines de la photographie archéologique : De Rome en Afrique* (Archives et histoire de l'archéologie 3). Drémil-Lafage, Mergoil.

ببليوغرافيا

برستد، جون هنري. 1900
Breasted, John Henry. 1900. *Egypt through the Stereoscope: A Journey through the Land of the Pharaohs*. New York, Underwood & Underwood.

بروفيرتس، جان-ميشيل. 1998
Bruffaerts, Jean-Michel. 1998. 'Une reine au pays de Toutankhamon'. *Museum Dynasticum* 10: 3–35.

بروفيرتس، جان-ميشيل. 2005
Bruffaerts, Jean-Michel. 2005. 'Un mastaba égyptien pour Bruxelles'. *Bulletin des Musées royaux d'art et d'histoire* 76: 5–36.

بروفيرتس، جان-ميشيل. 2006
Bruffaerts, Jean-Michel. 2006. 'Les coulisses d'un voyage royal : Le roi Albert et la reine Elisabeth en Égypte avec Jean Capart (1930)'. *Museum Dynasticum* 18: 28–49.

بروفيرتس، جان-ميشيل. 2022
Bruffaerts, Jean-Michel. 2022. *Jean Capart : Le chroniqueur de l'Égypte*. Brussels, Racine.

بروير، ماري-سيسيل ودويان، فلورانس. 2019
Bruwier, Marie-Cécile & Doyen, Florence (eds). 2019. *Héliopolis : La ville du soleil*. Brussels, Fondation Boghossian–Villa Empain.

كابارت، جان. 1901
Capart, Jean. 1901. 'En Égypte: Notes de voyage'. *Annales de la Société d'archéologie de Bruxelles. Mémoires, rapports et documents* 15: 153–181.

كابارت، جان. 1912
Capart, Jean. 1912. *Abydos : Le temple de Séti Iᵉʳ : Étude générale*. Brussels, Rossignol & Van den Bril.

كابارت، جان. 1923
Capart, Jean. 1923. *Toutankhamon*. Brussels, Vromant.

كابارت، جان. 1927
Capart, Jean. 1927. 'Rapport sur une fouille faite du 14 au 20 Février 1927 dans la nécropole de Héou'. *Annales du Service des Antiquités de l'Égypte* 27: 43–48.

كابارت، جان. 1928a
Capart, Jean. 1928a. 'Communication faite au Congrès des Orientalistes d'Oxford'. *Chronique d'Égypte* 4(7): 18–23.

كابارت، جان. 1928b
Capart, Jean. 1928b. 'Rapport du directeur : Exercice 1927–1928'. *Chronique d'Égypte* 4(7): 2–14.

كابارت، جان. 1929
Capart, Jean. 1929. 'Mission en Égypte : Janvier–Mars 1929'. *Chronique d'Égypte* 4(8): 189–191.

كابارت، جان. 1930a
Capart, Jean. 1930a. 'Coins ignorés d'Égypte'. *Chronique d'Égypte* 5(10): 180–188.

كابارت، جان. 1930b
Capart, Jean. 1930b. 'Visite officielle du Roi et de la Reine des Belges au Roi d'Égypte'. *Chronique d'Égypte* 5(10): 165–179.

كابارت، جان. 1932
Capart, Jean. 1932. 'Rapport du directeur : Exercice 1930–1931'. *Chronique d'Égypte* 7(13–14): 1–11.

كابارت، جان. 1940
Capart, Jean. 1940. 'Assemblée générale : Rapport du directeur'. *Chronique d'Égypte* 15(29): 13–16.

كابارت، جان. 1946
Capart, Jean. 1946. *Fouilles en Égypte : El Kab, impressions et souvenirs*. Brussels, Fondation Égyptologique Reine Élisabeth.

كابارت، جان. 1934
Capart, Jean & Marcelle Werbrouck. 1934. 'Lettres d'Égypte'. *Chronique d'Égypte* 9(18): 225–239.

كاراقّا، كوستانزا. 2011
Caraffa, Costanza. 2011. 'From "photo libraries" to "photo archives": On the epistemological potential of art-historical photo collections'. In: Caraffa, Constanza (ed.). *Photo Archives and the Photographic Memory of Art History (Italienische Forschungen des Kunsthistorischen Institutes in Florenz: I Mandorli 14)*. Berlin, Deutscher Kunstverlag: 11–44.

دي كايزر، أوجين. 1947
De Keyser, Eugénie. 1947. 'Jean Capart professeur et conférencier'. *Chronique d'Égypte* 22(44): 209–210.

دي ماير، مارلين؛ فانديرسميسن، يان؛ فيربروجن، كريستوف؛ كلايس، فوتر؛ ديلفو، لوك؛ بروير، ماري-سيسيل؛ كيرتينمونت، آرنو؛ فارمنبول، أوجين؛ بافيه لوران؛ فيليمز، هاركو. 2019
De Meyer, Marleen; Vandersmissen, Jan; Verbruggen, Christophe; Claes, Wouter; Delvaux, Luc; Bruwier, Marie-Cécile; Quertinmont, Arnaud; Warmenbol, Eugène; Bavay Laurent & Willems, Harco. 2019. 'Pyramids and progress: Belgian expansionism and the making of Egyptology, 1830–1952'. In: Navratilova, Hana; Gertzen, Thomas L.; Dodson, Aidan & Bednarski, Andrew (eds). *Towards a History of Egyptology: Proceedings of the Egyptological Section of the 8ᵗʰ ESHS Conference in London, 2018 (Investigatio Orientis 4)*. Münster, Zaphon: 173–193.

دي ماير، مارلين؛ بروفيرت، جان-ميشيل؛ فاندرسميسن، يان، 2023a
De Meyer, Marleen; Bruffaerts, Jean-Michel & Vandersmissen, Jan. 2023a. 'The Fondation Égyptologique Reine Élisabeth in Belgium and the creation of national and transnational Egyptological research infrastructures in the 1920s–1940s'. In: Matthes, Olaf & Gertzen, Tomas L. (eds) *Oriental Societies & Societal Self-Assertion: Associations, Funds and Societies for the Archaeological Exploration of the 'Ancient Near East'*. Münster, Zaphon.

دي ماير، مارلين؛ كلايس، فوتر؛ مهران، نهى؛ فان دير بير، أثينا؛ جريزر أوهارا، أود. 2023b
De Meyer, Marleen; Claes, Wouter; Mahran, Noha M.A.; Van der Perre, Athena & Gräzer Ohara, Aude. 2023b. 'Working with Capart: Quftis and local workmen during the Elkab excavation seasons, 1937–1946'. In: Navratilova, Hana; Gertzen, Thomas L.; De Meyer, Marleen; Dodson, Aidan M. & Bednarski, Andrew (eds). *Addressing Diversity. Inclusive Histories of Egyptology (Investigatio Orientis 9)*. Münster, Zaphon: 339–360.

دير مانويليان، بيتر. 1992
Der Manuelian, Peter. 1992. 'George Andrew Reisner on archaeological photography'. *Journal of the American Research Center in Egypt* 29: 1–34.

إدواردز، إليزابيث؛ هارت، جانيس. 2004
Edwards, Elizabeth & Hart, Janice. 2004. 'Photographs as objects'. In: Edwards, Elizabeth & Hart, Janice (eds) *Photographs Objects Histories: On the Materiality of Images*. London, Routledge: 1–15.

جريزر أوهارا، أود؛ ديلفو، لوك؛ فان دير بير، أثينا؛ دي ماير، مارلين؛ كلايس، فوتر. 2023
Gräzer Ohara, Aude; Delvaux, Luc; Van der Perre, Athena; De Meyer, Marleen & Claes, Wouter. 2023. 'Jean Capart, Neferirtenef et les mastabas perdus d'Auguste Mariette'. In: Podvin, Jean-Louis & Devauchelle, Didier (eds), *Actes du colloque « Mariette, deux siècles après »*. Boulogne-sur-Mer.

جريزر أوهارا، أود؛ ديلفو، لوك؛ فان دير بير، أثينا؛ دي ماير، مارلين؛ كلايس، فوتر. 2021
Gräzer Ohara, Aude; Van der Perre, Athena; De Meyer, Marleen & Claes, Wouter. 2021. 'Un demi-siècle d'égyptologie en images'. *Archéologia* 596: 18–19.

جرين، جون بيسلي. 1854
Greene, John Beasly. 1854. *Le Nil : Monuments, paysages, explorations photographiques*. Paris, Blanquart-Évrard.

جرين، جون بيسلي. 1855
Greene, John Beasly. 1855. *Fouilles exécutées à Thèbes dans l'année 1855 : Textes hiéroglyphiques et documents inédits*. Paris, Firmin-Didot.

همفريز، أندرو. 2014
Humphreys, Andrew. 2014. *Grand Hotels of Egypt in the Golden Age of Travel*. Cairo, American University in Cairo Press.

همفريز، أندرو. 2015
Humphreys, Andrew. 2015. *On the Nile in the Golden Age of Travel*. Cairo, American University in Cairo Press.

هوتنر، ميكايلا. 2016
Hüttner, Michaela. 2016. 'Geschichte der Fotografie: Die ersten 50 Jahre'. In: Haag, Sabine & Hüttner, Michaela (eds): *Von Alexandria nach Abu Simbel: Ägypten in frühen Fotografien*. Vienna, Kunsthistorisches Museum: 11–19.

كيمر، لودفيج. 1931
Keimer, Ludwig. 1931. 'L'égyptologie et les sciences naturelles'. *Chronique d'Égypte* 6(12) : 306–311.

لينرت، إيسولد. 2023
Lehnert, Isolde. 2023. 'An independent scholar and collector: Ludwig Keimer in Egypt'. In: Navratilova, Hana; Gertzen, Thomas L.; De Meyer, Marleen; Dodson, Aidan & Bednarski, Andrew (eds). *Addressing Diversity. Inclusive Histories of Egyptology (Investigatio Orientis 9)*. Münster, Zaphon: 73–108.

ليم، لوك. 2008
Limme, Luc. 2008. 'Elkab, 1937–2007: Seventy years of Belgian archaeological research'. *British Museum Studies in Ancient Egypt and Sudan* 9: 15–50.

مكفايدن، ليسلي؛ هيكس، دان. 2020
McFayden, Lesley & Hicks, Dan (eds). 2020. *Archaeology and Photography: Time, Objectivity and Archive*. London, Bloomsbury.

بيتري، ويليام ماثيو فليندرز. 1904
Petrie, William Matthew Flinders. 1904. *Methods and Aims in Archaeology*. London, Macmillan.

بياشنتيني، باترازيا. 2014
Piacentini, Patrizia. 2014. 'Theodor Kofler et les premières photographies aériennes des monuments égyptiens'. *Bulletin de la Société française d'Égyptologie* 190: 23–36.

بياشنتيني، باترازيا. 2015
Piacentini, Patrizia (ed.). 2015. *Egitto dal cielo, 1914: La riscoperta del fotografo pioniere, prigioniero, professionista Theodor Kofler / Egypt from the sky, 1914: The Rediscovery of the Photographer Pioneer, Prisoner, Professional Theodor Kofler*. Firenze, Phasar Edizioni.

1. Port of Alexandria

In 1909, Jean Capart travelled to Abydos to document the New Kingdom Temple of Seti I in preparation for a new book. Arriving in Egypt by boat, he photographed the bustling quay and custom house in the port of Alexandria, the latter flying the old Egyptian flag with a crescent and star. The activity at the landing place betrays the importance of Alexandria as a port city.

Jean Capart, 23 March 1909

Inv. EGI.01057

2. Sphinx at the Serapeum of Alexandria

Evaristo Breccia, director of the Graeco-Roman Museum of Alexandria (far right), poses in front of one of the sphinxes located near the triumphal column of Emperor Diocletian, also known as 'Pompey's Pillar', at the site of the Serapeum in Alexandria. He is in the company of Baudouin van de Walle (second from the left), Éléonore Bille-de Mot (middle), Marcelle Werbrouck (second from the right), and three students of Jean Capart.

Jean Capart, April 1925

Inv. EGI.05180

3. Temple of Amun, Tanis

Between 1929 and 1956, the site of Tanis in the Delta was excavated by the French mission directed by Pierre Montet. The monumental blocks and obelisks strewn about on the surface form the remnants of the ruined Temple of Amun. On top of the outcrop (left), stands the French excavation house. Women are among the Egyptian labourers. In the Delta region, it was and still is customary for both Egyptian men and women to work on excavations.

Jean Capart, January–February 1934

Inv. EGI.10023

4. *Sais* in the streets of Cairo

Two *Sais*, or running footmen, are seen in front of Hotel Le Bosphore in Cairo. *Sais* rented their services to wealthy Egyptians and tourists and ran alongside or in front of their horse-drawn carriages in order to clear the road. Generally, *Sais* came from the Delta and were dressed in a white shirt, short puffy trousers and an embroidered waistcoat.

Jean Capart, 4 December 1905–13 January 1906

Inv. EGI.00879

5. Obelisk of Senusret I, Heliopolis

Surrounded by fields, the obelisk of Senusret I is the only remaining monument still standing in its original position in the Temple of Re at Tell el-Hisn (ancient Heliopolis), once the largest solar cult complex in ancient Egypt. Two other obelisks originating from this temple are now in New York and London, and are often referred to as 'Cleopatra's needles'. In the foreground are the remains of the precinct wall of the 'Hyksos Fort', while the enclosure wall of Tell el-Hisn can be seen in the background.

Jean Capart, 15 April 1909

Inv. EGI.01178

6. Sayed 'Cid' Mahmud at el-Marg

At the request of the Belgian entrepreneur Édouard Empain, who was to build a new suburb in Heliopolis, northeast of Cairo, Jean Capart excavated part of the 6,000-plus-acre area to make sure no archaeological remains were present there. During his exploration of the region, Capart was often accompanied by Sayed 'Cid' Mahmud, whom he portrays here sitting on a donkey on the road to the village of el-Marg.

Jean Capart, 13 February–mid April 1907

Inv. EGI.01148

7. Villagers in the area of Heliopolis

Sayed 'Cid' Mahmud on his donkey passes a group of Egyptian women carrying on their heads water jars filled from a nearby well. They are walking back to their village, visible in the background.

Charles Mathien, 13 February–mid April 1907

Inv. EGI.06013

8. Construction of Heliopolis

With the creation of the Cairo Electric Railways and Heliopolis Oases Company by Édouard Empain and his Egyptian partner Boghos Nubar Pasha in 1906, the urban project of Masr el-Gedida (New Cairo) was launched. An entire new city was built in a deserted area northeast of Cairo. Jean Capart captured the levelling works for the construction of roads in the future residential area of this new city named Heliopolis.

Jean Capart, 13 February–mid April 1907

Inv. EGI.01119

9. Construction of Heliopolis

Villas and other buildings were constructed in the so-called 'Heliopolis style', an architectural style that combined elements of Egyptian, Moorish, Persian, European and Neoclassical traditions to form a homogeneous unit. The domed building on the right is the casino under construction, along with several residential units lining the Ramsis and Boutros Ghali streets. Like the famous Heliopolis Palace Hotel, the casino was turned into a military hospital during both World Wars.

Jean Capart (?), 15 April 1909

Inv. EGI.01338

10. Construction of Heliopolis

Villas under construction on the western outskirts of Heliopolis. This photograph was taken from one of the stations, probably el-Qubba, along the railway that connected el-Matariya with downtown Cairo. To the right of the casino (domed building in the background, left) are the towered buildings of Abbas Street (currently Boulevard Ibrahim el-Laqqany).

Jean Capart, 15 April 1909

Inv. EGI.01324

11. Qasr el-Baron under construction, Heliopolis

Baron Édouard Empain commissioned the French architect Alexandre Marcel to build a Hindu-style palace as his private residence. Known as the 'Qasr el-Baron', it remains an important landmark in Cairo's present-day urban landscape. Prior to its completion in 1911, Jean Capart photographed its construction in 1909, with (in the foreground) the tramline of the future el-Sultan Hussein Street.

Jean Capart, 15 April 1909

Inv. EGI.01336

12. Excavations at Heliopolis

Jean Capart set up camp in the desert of Abbasiya to carry out test excavations in the area where the new city of Heliopolis was to be constructed. On 13 February 1907, Capart arrived at the location with his Egyptian team, Charles Mathien (centre, man wearing a dark three-piece suit) and four camels carrying their equipment. Fernand Mayence (probably the man wearing a pith helmet, right) had already set up the tents.

Jean Capart, 13 February 1907

Inv. EGI.01052

13. Excavations at Heliopolis

At full capacity, more than 250 Egyptian workmen were employed by Jean Capart and his team at Heliopolis: trained excavators, basket carriers, guards and camp personnel. Some are known by name, such as Ismail Salem (a), Sayed 'Cid' Mahmud (c), or Abd el-Latif Salem, one of the overseers of the workmen (d). The *reis* (b; name unknown) organised the work of the Egyptian labourers at the excavation, assisted by Abd el-Latif Salem and at least four other overseers (e; names unknown).

Jean Capart, 13 February–19 March 1907

Inv. EGI.01063 (a), EGI.01064 (b), EGI.06030 (c), EGI.01159 (d), EGI.01109 (e)

14. Excavations at Heliopolis

Abd el-Latif Salem, one of the overseers of the workmen, and Jean Capart supervise the excavation of a large trench in the desert of Abbasiya. The excavators' camp is visible in the background, with, from left to right, the three tents of the archaeologists, the small tent for the toilet, and the kitchen tent with its stove.

Charles Mathien (?), 13 February–19 March 1907

Inv. EGI.01094

15. Excavations at Heliopolis

A Bedouin man armed with a rifle stands guard, while the French geologist and archaeologist Jules Couyat-Barthoux of the Service de la Carte Géologique de France and Jean Capart undertake a geological survey in the desert of Abbasiya.

Photographer unknown, March 1907

Inv. EGI.01124

16. Excavations at Heliopolis

A water carrier unloads his camel to supply the camp with fresh water, which was kept in a *zir* (water jar) in front of one of the tents. In the background, a group of Egyptian workmen are excavating.

Jean Capart, 13 February–19 March 1907

Inv. EGI.01031

17. Excavations at Heliopolis

The Egyptian cook prepares a meal on the stove of his kitchen tent. The man seated next to him is most probably Abdallah, one of the *sufragis* in the team. The excavators' tents are visible in the background.

Jean Capart, 13 February–19 March 1907

Inv. EGI.06029

18. Excavations at Heliopolis

An unidentified Egyptian man (perhaps a notable from a nearby village?) poses with a workman in front of one of the camp's tents.

Jean Capart, 13 February–19 March 1907

Inv. EGI.06015

19. Excavations at Heliopolis

A look inside one of the tents that served as a bedroom in the excavators' camp.

Jean Capart, 13 February–19 March 1907

Inv. EGI.01114

20. Excavations at Heliopolis

Abdallah guards the tent that served as a dining room, in front of which Jean Capart (left) and another Western man (right, probably Fernand Mayence) are seated on folding chairs reading a newspaper. The large jar on a stand is a *zir* (water jar).

Charles Mathien (?), 13 February–19 March 1907

Inv. EGI.06033

21. Excavations at Heliopolis

From an archaeological perspective, the mission at Heliopolis proved to be a major disappointment, as nothing was found after more than four weeks of digging. On 19 March 1907, the camp of Jean Capart's team was dismantled. Several Egyptian workmen are gathering tools, while Ange Abela, the dragoman or interpreter, is seated among piles of baskets. In the background, Capart is talking to two workmen.

Charles Mathien (?), 19 March 1907

Inv. EGI.01092

22. Excavations at Heliopolis

The tableware used by the excavators is carefully packed into crates and padded with straw. Ange Abela, the dragoman or interpreter (standing, right), keeps a watchful eye.

Jean Capart, 19 March 1907

Inv. EGI.01033

23. Excavations at Heliopolis

Jean Capart dismantles his tent with the help of Abd el-Latif Salem, one of the overseers of the workmen (centre) and Abdallah, the man wearing a tarbush (right), who was probably a *sufragi*. Note the pile of empty wine and cognac bottles outside the tent (bottom left).

Charles Mathien (?), 19 March 1907

Inv. EGI.01211

24. Desert landscape at Abu Rawash

The desert landscape at Abu Rawash looking south, with the Giza pyramids on the horizon. The photograph was probably taken from the plateau where the 4th Dynasty pyramid of Djedefre is located.

Jean Capart, 25 January–7 April 1927

Inv. EGI.06203

25. Tramline to Giza

The tramline next to Pyramid Road or Sharia el-Haram connected central Cairo to the desert plateau of the Giza pyramids. The tramway ended at the Mena House, a former Khedivial hunting lodge built at the foot of the Giza plateau and serving as a hotel since 1886.

Jean Capart, January–March 1929

Inv. EGI.03928

26. Village of Nazlet el-Samman

The village of Nazlet el-Samman was once a small rural community in the shade of the Giza pyramids; today, it is part of the Cairo metropolis. Located at the base of Egypt's major tourism attraction, the village depended then and now on the income of tourists visiting the Old Kingdom necropolis of Giza.

Jean Capart, February–April 1907

Inv. EGI.01202

27. Village of Nazlet el-Samman

An Egyptian man walks down a path running between the houses of the village of Nazlet el-Samman and the eastern escarpment of the Giza plateau. It leads to the rock-cut tombs LG 76–80, which are visible in the background. They were excavated by the German Egyptologist Karl Richard Lepsius in 1842–1843.

Jean Capart, after 1906

Inv. EGI.01208

28. Abd el-Rahim at his house, Nazlet el-Samman

In the notes and diaries of Jean Capart, the name of Abd el-Rahim is frequently mentioned. He accompanied Capart to antiquity dealers and became a close acquaintance of his. Capart has here photographed him (centre, looking at the camera), together with several young boys (his sons?) and other men, in front of his house in the village of Nazlet el-Samman, near the pyramids of Giza.

Jean Capart, 10 or 25 April 1909

Inv. EGI.01234

29. Pyramid of Khufu, Giza

Abd el-Rahim poses in front of a large block at the base of the pyramid of Khufu. This block is part of the smooth outer casing that once covered the pyramid entirely. Several mastaba tombs of the so-called Western Cemetery can be recognised in the background. This image was taken on the north face of the pyramid, in which the entrance to the interior passageways is also located.

Jean Capart, January–March 1929

Inv. EGI.04024

30. Pyramid of Khufu, Giza

The upper courses of limestone blocks near the top of the pyramid of Khufu, on its west face. Part of the Mena House, a former Khedivial hunting lodge converted into a hotel in 1886, is visible at the foot of the pyramid. In the background, the Bahr el-Libeini, a canal crossing the cultivated plain, and a small village can be recognised.

Jean Capart, January–March 1929

Inv. EGI.03963

31. Pyramid of Khufu, Giza

The granite sarcophagus of Khufu located in the king's chamber inside his pyramid. The sarcophagus lid has long disappeared. The western and northern walls of the chamber are covered with graffiti by modern visitors.

Photographer unknown, no date

Inv. EGI.01215

32. Great Sphinx, Giza

Frontal view of the Great Sphinx, still largely buried beneath the desert sand. A creature with the body of a lion and the face of the Egyptian Pharaoh Khafre, it guards his pyramid, visible in the background. Jean Capart poses atop the sphinx's right forepaw.

Charles Mathien (?), 11 December 1905

Inv. EGI.00953

33. Great Sphinx, Giza

From 1925 onwards, a team directed by the French architect Émile Baraize cleared the Great Sphinx from the desert sand and restored it on behalf of the Service des Antiquités de l'Égypte. The workmen have constructed scaffolding upon the sphinx in order to carry out this work. In the background, the cultivated plain is visible, forming a natural border between the Giza Plateau and the western outskirts of Cairo.

Baudouin van de Walle, 1926

Inv. EGI.05619

34. Giza plateau

View south from the top of the pyramid of Khufu towards the so-called Central Field Cemetery. Émile Baraize's team was still clearing the Great Sphinx, its temple and the valley temple of the pyramid complex of Khafre, while Egyptian Egyptologist Selim Hassan was excavating the mastaba complex of Rawer. Most of the Central Field is still covered with sand, including the large tomb structure of Queen Khentkawes I. Muslim and Coptic cemeteries are located at the foot of Gebel el-Qibli in the centre. Unbeknownst to Capart, the workmen's village of the Giza necropolis (Heit el-Ghurab) would be excavated decades later in that same area. On the horizon, the pyramid sites of Abusir and Saqqara can be seen on the left, with Dahshur visible on the right.

Jean Capart, January–March 1929

35. Giza plateau

This view from the top of the pyramid of Khufu shows the mastaba tombs of Cemetery GIS along the southern base of the pyramid. These tombs date for the most part to the 4th Dynasty and were excavated by a German-Austrian mission led by Hermann Junker between 1925 and 1929. Note the Decauville railways to the right, which were used to transport debris from the excavations.

Jean Capart, January–March 1929

Inv. EGI.03965

36. Giza plateau

View from the top of the pyramid of Khufu, which casts its shadow upon the rest house of Khedive Ismail (occupying its northeastern corner), as well as upon part of the village of Nazlet el-Samman and the golf course. The rest house was demolished by King Faruq in 1944, who a few years later would build his own in the same location. In the background, the Bahr el-Libeini and el-Muhit canals run across the cultivated plain, with the tramline and Pyramid Road or Sharia el-Haram to the left.

Jean Capart, January–March 1929

Inv. EGI.03962

37. Pyramid complex of Menkaure, Giza

Marcelle Werbrouck (right) sits next to Marguerite Thirionet on a wall of the Pyramid Temple of Menkaure. This 4th Dynasty pyramid is the smallest of the three Giza pyramids, built by a grandson of Khufu.

Jean Capart, January–March 1929

Inv. EGI.03943

38. Khentkawes pyramid town, Giza

Located east of the pyramid complex of Menkaure, this Old Kingdom town housed the priests who served in the funerary cult of Queen Khentkawes I. Built of mudbrick, these houses were carefully planned and constructed along a street. This area was excavated in 1932–1933 by Egyptian Egyptologist Selim Hassan, whom Jean Capart has photographed here, standing at the front of a group of people in the ancient street.

Jean Capart, January–February 1934

Inv. EGI.10035

39. Tomb of Queen Khentkawes I, Giza

The tomb of Queen Khentkawes I lies in the Central Field Cemetery to the southwest of the Great Sphinx. Often referred to as the 'Fourth Pyramid', her tomb was in fact a two-stepped structure and not an actual pyramid. Dated to the end of the 4th into the early 5th Dynasty, it was the last funerary royal monument built at Giza. The rope-tied blocks in the foreground are fragments of the pink granite door jambs of the tomb's chapel, bearing the name and titles of the queen.

Jean Capart, January–February 1934

Inv. EGI.10039

40. Old Kingdom rock-cut tombs, Giza

Marguerite Thirionet and Abd el-Rahim stand in front of a number of rock-cut tombs to the east of the pyramid of Khufu. The village of Nazlet el-Samman ran right up to them and one of its modern houses can be seen on the right, constructed in rough mud-plastered limestone blocks. These tombs were excavated by Ahmed Fakhry between 1932 and 1934, and thus freshly exposed when Jean Capart photographed them in 1934.

Jean Capart, January–February 1934

Inv. EGI.10041

41. Campbell's Tomb, Giza

An Egyptian man stands in the southeastern corner of the large burial shaft of tomb LG 84 at Giza, also known as Campbell's Tomb. It is the largest and easternmost of the Late Period tombs of the Central Field Cemetery and was named after Patrick Campbell, a Scottish diplomat and army officer who assisted the British explorer Howard Vyse at the Giza pyramids and cemeteries in 1837.

Jean Capart, 11 December 1905

Inv. EGI.00952

42. Northern pyramid, Zawiyat el-Aryan

a	b
c	d

Two unfinished pyramids dominate the site of Zawiyat el-Aryan. The northern one or so-called 'Great Pit' was built by an unknown ruler of the 4th Dynasty. Its main feature is a long descending passage that leads to the burial chamber where an unusual oval sarcophagus was found. Jean Capart visited the site at least twice: in 1907, in the company of Franz Cumont and Charles Mathien (holding a walking stick; d) and again in 1927, with Marcelle Werbrouck and Capart's wife Marguerite Thirionet (dressed in white; b–c).

Jean Capart, 26 March–3 April 1907 (d), 25 January–7 April 1927 (a–c)   Inv. EGI.06208 (a), EGI.06209 (b), EGI.06210 (c), EGI.00867 (d)

43. Northern pyramid, Zawiyat el-Aryan

The pyramids of Zawiyat el-Aryan were excavated by Alexandre Barsanti on behalf of the Service des Antiquités de l'Égypte in 1905–1906. Barsanti and his team revealed the sarcophagus that was sunk into the pavement of the burial chamber, and removed several of the large granite blocks to in vain search for additional passageways and chambers. Here, Franz Cumont (left) and Charles Mathien are posing between the oval lid of the sarcophagus and some of the removed blocks.

Jean Capart, 26 March–3 April 1907

Inv. EGI.01183

44. Jean Capart in the desert between Abusir and Giza

Jean Capart seated on a donkey, with the pyramids of Giza in the background. From left to right: the pyramids of Menkaure, Khafre and Khufu. This photograph was taken on an excursion after the excavation season at Heliopolis.

Charles Mathien (?), 26 March–3 April 1907

Inv. EGI.01154

45. Sun temple of Niuserre, Abu Ghurab

Jean Capart poses seated on the remains of a mudbrick imitation of a solar boat, the function of which was to carry the sun god and the deceased pharaoh through the netherworld. It is located to the south of the sun temple of the 5th Dynasty king Niuserre, the best preserved of the known Old Kingdom sun temples of ancient Egypt close to Abusir.

Charles Mathien (?), 6 December 1905–11 January 1906

Inv. EGI.05742 (reproduction of a photographic print)

46. Pyramid complex of Neferirkare, Abusir

Between 1902 and 1908, German Egyptologist Ludwig Borchardt and his team of the Deutsche Orient-Gesellschaft excavated the 5th Dynasty necropolis at Abusir. In 1907, Jean Capart visited the site and photographed their work at the pyramid complex of King Neferirkare, showing the ruler's cleared mortuary temple at the foot of the pyramid.

Jean Capart, 26 March–3 April 1907

Inv. EGI.01028

47. Pyramid complex of Neferirkare, Abusir

During the excavation, rubble was carted off by Decauville railways, creating long rows of spoil heaps, as seen in the foreground. On the horizon, from left to right, the pyramids of Teti and Userkaf, and the Step Pyramid of Djoser at Saqqara can be recognised.

Jean Capart, 26 March–3 April 1907

Inv. EGI.01186

48. Excavation house of Auguste Mariette, North Saqqara

Franz Cumont (left) and Charles Mathien are standing on the spoil heaps to the northwest of the pyramid complex of Djoser. In the background stands the excavation house of the famous French Egyptologist Auguste Mariette, the founder of the Service des Antiquités de l'Égypte (1858) and the Bulaq Museum (1863). Mariette worked at over thirty-five sites in Egypt, including Saqqara, where he made many important discoveries, notably the Serapeum.

Jean Capart, 26 March–3 April 1907

Inv. EGI.01113

49. Serapeum, North Saqqara

Franz Cumont stands next to one of the Greek-style statues that adorned the northern wall of the dromos leading to the Serapeum, here buried beneath the sand. The Serapeum was the subterranean burial place of the sacred Apis bulls, and was excavated in 1850–1851 by Auguste Mariette. During the Ptolemaic Period, eleven statues of Greek poets and philosophers were added to the complex.

Jean Capart, 26 March–3 April 1907

Inv. EGI.01181

50. Tomb of Ti, North Saqqara

Relief decoration inside the Old Kingdom mastaba tomb of Ti, a high official of the 5th Dynasty. It shows the deceased and his wife attending the cattle count, which was a way of evaluating taxes in ancient Egypt. Ti was overseer of several pyramid complexes and sun temples, and his is one of the finest decorated tombs at Saqqara.

Jean Capart, 26 March–3 April 1907

Inv. EGI.01195

51. Tomb of Mereruka, North Saqqara

Detail of the carved decoration, with fine interior detail work, on the southern facade of the mastaba tomb of Mereruka, showing the deceased and part of his titles. Mereruka was a vizier, chief justice, and inspector of the priests of the pyramid of Teti (6th Dynasty). A son-in-law of the king, his mastaba tomb contains thirty-two rooms and is one of the largest in the Saqqara necropolis.

Jean Capart, 25 January–7 April 1927

Inv. EGI.06181

52. Pyramid complex of Teti, North Saqqara

Fragment of a block bearing the hieroglyphic sign of the hare, found among the remains of the Pyramid Temple of Teti, first ruler of the 6th Dynasty. The subterranean chambers of Teti's pyramid were inscribed with Pyramid Texts, a set of more than 800 spells that are the earliest known religious funerary texts of ancient Egypt.

Jean Capart, 25 January–7 April 1927

Inv. EGI.06187

53. Gisr el-Nehas, North Saqqara

Northern face of the monumental mudbrick wall at Saqqara, known as the Gisr el-Nehas, located east of the pyramid complex of Teti. The large opening in the wall was cleared by James Edward Quibell and his team in 1905 on behalf of the Service des Antiquités de l'Égypte. A number of late Roman tombs, one containing a stone sarcophagus, are visible in the foreground.

Jean Capart, 6 December 1905–10 January 1906

Inv. EGI.05571

54. Pyramid complex of Djoser, North Saqqara

Djoser's pyramid complex was the first royal monument in Egypt built entirely of stone. In 1927, Jean Capart was guided around the site by British Egyptologist Cecil M. Firth, who was excavating there on behalf of the Service des Antiquités de l'Égypte. This view from the top of the Step Pyramid shows the eastern portion of this funerary complex, surrounded by the large spoil heaps from Firth's excavations.

Jean Capart, 25 January–7 April 1927

Inv. EGI.06133

55. Pyramid complex of Djoser, North Saqqara

View of the entrance gate and colonnade leading to the south court of the Step Pyramid of Djoser. The seated man holding a dog is British Egyptologist Battiscombe G. Gunn, who was then excavating, together with Cecil M. Firth, the Teti pyramid cemeteries just northeast of the Step Pyramid.

Baudouin van de Walle, 1926

Inv. EGI.05644

56. Mastaba of Neferirtenef, North Saqqara

In the winter of 1905, Jean Capart travelled to Saqqara to acquire the funerary chapel of an Old Kingdom tomb, for the Egyptian collection of the Brussels museum. James Edward Quibell of the Service des Antiquités de l'Égypte proposed different monuments to Capart, who finally selected the mastaba tomb of Neferirtenef, a high official of the 5th Dynasty. Prior to dismantling and packing, each block of the decorated chapel was numbered.

James Edward Quibell, 3–15 January 1906   Inv. EGI.00092 (reproduction of a photographic print)

57. Mastaba of Neferirtenef, North Saqqara

The dismantling, transport and reconstruction of the mastaba of Neferirtenef in Brussels was financed by the Belgian industrialist Édouard Empain. Here, two workmen are packing the dismantled blocks into small individual wooden crates, for their safe transport to Brussels. Below and next to the hoist lie two large wooden boxes containing the false-door stelae of Neferirtenef's funerary chapel.

James Edward Quibell, 3–15 January 1906

Inv. EGI.00094 (reproduction of a photographic print)

58. Mastaba of Netjeruser, North Saqqara

Upon Jean Capart's arrival at Saqqara, James Edward Quibell and his team were already clearing two mastabas. This photograph probably shows the excavation of the mastaba of Netjeruser, which was rejected by Capart who considered its decoration too repetitive. In 1907–1908, this mastaba was acquired by the American collector Edward E. Ayer, who offered it to the Field Museum of Natural History in Chicago.

Jean Capart or Charles Mathien, 6 December 1905

Inv. EGI.00980

59. Mastaba of Neferirtenef, North Saqqara

An old *reis*, whose name is unknown, assisted Jean Capart in his search for a mastaba. As a child, he had worked with Auguste Mariette in the Saqqara necropolis and he remembered that in 1860 the beautifully decorated mastaba of Neferirtenef had been discovered southeast of the pyramid complex of Djoser. Following his instructions, the mastaba was relocated on 13 December 1905 and approved by Capart (here wearing a dark coat and a pith helmet). The old *reis* is most probably the man to his left holding a walking stick.

Charles Mathien (?), 13 December 1905

Inv. EGI.00984

60. Mastaba of Neferirtenef, Brussels

a	b
c	d

In May 1906, the wooden boxes containing the blocks of the mastaba of Neferirtenef arrived in Brussels. From the train station of Brussels-Luxembourg, they were transported by horse and cart to the museum.

Photographer unknown, May 1906

Inv. EGI.01523 (a), EGI.01526 (b), EGI.01529 (c), EGI.01525 (d)

61. Mastaba of Neferirtenef, Brussels

a	b
c	d

All available hands of the museum staff, both men and women, were called to help move the cases into the museum rooms where the funerary chapel was to be reconstructed. To this day, it remains a masterpiece of the Egyptian collection of the Royal Museums of Art and History (E.02465).

Photographer unknown, May 1906

Inv. EGI.01530 (a), EGI.01534 (b), EGI.01535 (c), EGI.01533 (d)

62. Landscape, North Saqqara

A large residual lake formed at the desert edge of the Saqqara Plateau, after the receding of the Nile's annual flood. Egyptian men are fetching water from the lake, while their camels sit on the embankment and a donkey quenches its thirst. In the background, the Step Pyramid of Djoser is visible.

Jean Capart, 6 December 1905

Inv. EGI.00978

63. Middle Kingdom pyramid complex, South Saqqara

This undulating wall served as the enclosure wall of an unfinished pyramid complex built for an unidentified pharaoh of the late Middle Kingdom. The site was excavated by a team of the Service des Antiquités de l'Égypte directed by Gustave Jéquier. Part of the necropolis of Dahshur is visible on the horizon with, from left to right, the pyramids of Senusret III and Amenemhat III, and the Bent Pyramid of Snefru.

Jean Capart, 1 April 1930

Inv. EGI.07366

64. Settlement site of Memphis, Mit Rahina

An Egyptian man stands in the unexcavated ruins of Kom el-Qala, which are part of Memphis, the first capital of pharaonic Egypt. Much of ancient Memphis lies beneath thick layers of Nile alluvium, making it difficult or almost impossible to excavate. At Kom el-Qala, important monuments were discovered, such as the palace of Pharaoh Merenptah and a temple dedicated to Ptah.

Jean Capart, 6 December 1905

Inv. EGI.00968

65. Colossal statue of Ramesses II, Mit Rahina

Head of a monumental limestone statue of Ramesses II. Over 10 metres tall, it was first excavated in 1821 near the south gate of the large temple complex of Ptah at Kom el-Qala by the Italian Giovanni Battista Belzoni. In 1902, the Service des Antiquités de l'Égypte rebuilt a wooden and mudbrick shelter around it. Today, the statue is a major highlight of the open-air museum in Mit Rahina.

Jean Capart, after 1902

Inv. EGI.01180

66. Alabaster Sphinx, Mit Rahina

This large alabaster sphinx represents an unidentified pharaoh of the New Kingdom and was discovered in 1911–1912 by Ernest Mackay, an assistant to William Matthew Flinders Petrie, within the enclosure of the large temple complex of Ptah in the area of Kom el-Qala. In 1913, it was placed upright, but upon a higher base of ancient blocks, to protect it from the resurgent groundwater.

Jean Capart, April 1925

Inv. EGI.05353

67. Landscape near Dahshur

This photograph taken in the area of Dahshur shows the Nile with on its west bank the Bent Pyramid and the Red Pyramid. Both pyramids were built by Pharaoh Snefru and date to the beginning of the 4th Dynasty. This same pharaoh first built another pyramid earlier in his reign, at the site of Meidum further south.

Jean Capart, around 8 April 1909

Inv. EGI.01274

68. Pyramid complex of Snefru, Meidum

When excavating at Tell Hiw in 1927, Jean Capart visited for the first time the site of Meidum, together with the other team members. This photograph shows Marcelle Werbrouck (right) and an unidentified woman in the desert, with the pyramid of Snefru in the background. The sloping mounds of debris are the remains of the pyramid's outer casing and fill.

Jean Capart, 25 January–7 April 1927

Inv. EGI.06166

69. Pyramid complex of Snefru, Meidum

During the royal voyage of 1930, Jean Capart returned to Meidum in the company of Elisabeth, Queen of the Belgians. On 31 March, they were received by Alan Rowe (right), director of the Eckley B. Coxe Expedition for the University Museum of Pennsylvania, who was excavating the pyramid of Snefru. The Queen and Alan Rowe stand here on the rock-cut causeway leading to the mortuary temple at the base of Snefru's pyramid.

Paul Polinet, 31 March 1930

Inv. EGI.07554 (reproduction of a photographic print)

70. Temple of Soknopaios, Dimai

The crocodile god Sobek was worshipped in many temples across the Fayum. At Soknopaiou Nesos (modern Dimai), a large temple was built in the Ptolemaic period and dedicated to Soknopaios, a local version of Sobek. This photograph shows Marguerite Thirionet amongst the ruins of the main temple. Part of the large mudbrick temenos wall is still standing in the background.

Jean Capart, January–February 1934

Inv. EGI.10002

71. Temple of Sobek, Qasr Qarun

Marguerite Thirionet and an Egyptian man stand in front of the Ptolemaic temple dedicated to Sobek at Qasr Qarun, located on the western edge of Birket (Lake) Qarun in the Fayum. From Qasr Qarun, an important caravan route connected the Fayum with the Bahariya Oasis. The photograph shows the temple prior to its restoration in 2009 by the Egyptian Antiquities Service.

Jean Capart, January–February 1934

Inv. EGI.10011

72. Pedestals of Amenemhat III, Biahmu

Kheir Aballah, a local inhabitant of Biahmu (Fayum), stands between the large blocks of one of the pedestals that once held colossal quartzite statues of Pharaoh Amenemhat III. These two statues once stood on the shores of Lake Moeris, but have long since disappeared.

Jean Capart, January–February 1934

Inv. EGI.010018

73. Pedestals of Amenemhat III, Biahmu

Marguerite Thirionet stands on one of the blocks of the ruined eastern pedestal at Biahmu (Fayum). To her left, a group of Egyptians stand in front of the remains of a large stone wall that once surrounded the pedestal.

Jean Capart, January–February 1934

74. Monument of Senusret I, Abgig

Marguerite Thirionet stands atop fragments of a red granite monument erected by Pharaoh Senusret I at Abgig in the Fayum. This free-standing structure was originally almost 13 metres high, with a rounded top and inscribed on all four sides. It remained intact in its original position up until the mid-18th century, when it collapsed into pieces. In the 1970s, it was finally restored and re-erected on a square in Medinet el-Fayum.

Jean Capart, January–February 1934

Inv. EGI.10015

75. Bahr Yussef, Medinet el-Fayum

The origins of Medinet el-Fayum, the largest town of the Fayum, date back to prehistoric times when people settled on the shores of Lake Moeris, a large freshwater lake that today persists as Birket Qarun. This lake was fed by the Bahr Yussef, an offshoot of the Nile that is pictured here flowing through the town of Medinet el-Fayum. During the 12th Dynasty, various pharaohs enlarged the Bahr Yussef and turned it into a canal controlled by a series of dams, allowing for the irrigation of the oasis's agricultural land.

Jean Capart, January–February 1934

Inv. EGI.10014

76. Temple of Herishef, Ihnasiya el-Medina

The temple of the god Herishef at Ihnasiya el-Medina (Herakleopolis Magna), close to the entrance to the Fayum, is largely destroyed down to its foundations, with only a few decorated blocks remaining in place in the portico pictured here. The blocks are inscribed with the name of New Kingdom Pharaoh Ramesses II. Marguerite Thirionet sits on one of the six granite column bases of the portico, while a group of Egyptian villagers stands to her right.

Jean Capart, January–February 1934

Inv. EGI.09982

77. Temple of Ramesses II, Ihnasiya el-Medina

The entrance gate and columns of the small Temple of Ramesses II at Kom el-Aqarib, located southeast of the Temple of Herishef at Ihnasiya el-Medina. The blocks were reused from an earlier, Middle Kingdom sanctuary and bear the names of Queen Sobekneferu and Senusret III. Marguerite Thirionet stands before the southern pillar of the entrance gate, while an Egyptian man stands nearby.

Jean Capart, January–February 1934

Inv. EGI.09981

78. Boats on the Nile, Middle Egypt

Two wooden sailing boats or *feluccas* on the Nile with their sails unfurled, somewhere in Middle Egypt.

Jean Capart, 6 or 7 April 1909

Inv. EGI.01297

79. Sheikh Fadl, Middle Egypt

During the royal voyage of 1930, the yacht *Khassed Kheir*, placed at the disposal of Belgian Queen Elisabeth and her entourage by Egyptian King Fuad I, was welcomed throughout the country by enthusiastic crowds of people. This festively decorated boat flying both the Egyptian and Belgian flags greeted the royal yacht at Sheikh Fadl in Middle Egypt. Jean Capart describes in his diary that an orchestra played the *Brabançonne*, the national anthem of Belgium, as they passed by.

Paul Polinet, 15 March 1930

Inv. EGI.07550 (reproduction of a photographic print)

80. Funeral, Middle Egypt

A group of Egyptian women dressed in black and children cross the fields on their way back from a funeral. The photograph was taken at an unknown location in Middle Egypt.

Jean Capart, 3–6 April 1909

Inv. EGI.01239

81. Temple of Ramesses II, Sheikh Ibada

Prior to the royal voyage of 1930, Jean Capart and his wife Marguerite Thirionet were invited to join a Nile cruise organised by the Goldman family, their American friends. With Capart as their guide, they explored sites rarely visited by Western tourists. This photograph shows Marguerite standing in the hypostyle hall of the Temple of Ramesses II at Sheikh Ibada (Antinoöpolis), together with Julius Goldman (centre) and his son-in-law Bernhard Gutmann (right).

Jean Capart, 24 January 1930

Inv. EGI.07134

82. Temple of Amun, el-Ashmunein

Two Egyptian men and four of Jean Capart's travel companions, including Marguerite Thirionet (standing to the left) and Marcelle Werbrouck (seated in the middle), pictured between the columns of the peristyle court in the Temple of Amun at el-Ashmunein (Hermopolis Magna). The entrance gate of the temple's pylon, visible in the background, was constructed using *talatat* blocks from the temples of nearby Amarna.

Jean Capart, 25 January–7 April 1927

Inv. EGI.06219

83. Basilica, el-Ashmunein

An Egyptian man poses in front of the ruins of the Coptic basilica at el-Ashmunein (Hermopolis Magna) dating back to the 5th century CE. The columns in the background, crowned with Corinthian capitals, originally belonged to a Greek-style Ptolemaic temple.

Jean Capart, 12 November 1945

Inv. EGI.12147

84. Tomb of Petosiris, Tuna el-Gebel

Detail of the interior reliefs decorating an intercolumnar wall of the pronaos within the tomb chapel of Petosiris, a high priest of Thoth at Hermopolis Magna who lived during the 4th century BCE. This tomb is famous for its well-preserved facade shaped as an Egyptian temple, as well as for its decoration combining traditional Egyptian themes with a Hellenistic style, as seen in these scenes depicting carpenters and perfume-makers.

Jean Capart, 25 January–7 April 1927

85. Tomb of Petosiris, Tuna el-Gebel

The horned altar in the open space in front of the tomb of Petosiris is also built in a Hellenistic style. In the background, a group of donkey-drivers and *ghafirs* (guards) await Jean Capart and his travel party.

Jean Capart, 25 January–7 April 1927

Inv. EGI.06213

86. Tomb of Governor Djehutihotep, Deir el-Bersha

During his voyages through Egypt, Jean Capart visited many sites well off the beaten track, such as Deir el-Bersha, a necropolis in Middle Egypt where Middle Kingdom governors were buried. Most rock-cut tombs there have collapsed due to earthquakes and later quarrying, and that of Governor Djehutihotep, dating back to the 12th Dynasty, remains the best preserved one. Capart took a rare early photograph of this tomb's facade.

Jean Capart, January–February 1934

Inv. EGI.09880

87. Tomb of Governor Nehri I, Deir el-Bersha

Marcelle Werbrouck leans on a decorated block in the tomb of Middle Kingdom Governor Nehri I at Deir el-Bersha. The tomb chapel is heavily damaged, but this block preserves a relief of men wrestling.

Jean Capart, January–February 1934

Inv. EGI.09884

88. Central City, Amarna

In 1934, Jean Capart spent two weeks at Amarna (Akhetaten), where John D.S. Pendlebury and his team from the Egypt Exploration Society were excavating in the Central City. This photograph shows their work in the area east of the King's House, perhaps in the mudbrick buildings of the *Per-ankh* ('House of Life') and the Records Office. In the latter building, most of the cuneiform tablets or so-called Amarna Letters had been found.

Jean Capart, January 1934

Inv. EGI.09867

89. Central City, Amarna

Marcelle Werbrouck overlooks the southwestern row of storerooms that were part of the King's House of Akhenaten, located in the Central City at Amarna. They were excavated by John D.S. Pendlebury and his team during their excavation campaign of 1931–1932 on behalf of the Egypt Exploration Society.

Jean Capart, January 1934

Inv. EGI.09824

90. Excavation house, Amarna

Marguerite Thirionet (left), Marcelle Werbrouck (petting a dog), and Marcelle Baud stand in the inner courtyard of the North Expedition House of the Egypt Exploration Society. Located in the North City of Amarna, it was built on the spot where ancient house U25.11 had originally stood. John D.S. Pendlebury and his team used this expedition house during their archaeological campaign of 1933–1934.

Jean Capart, January 1934

Inv. EGI.09830

91. Excavation house, Amarna

Jean Capart photographed not only the excavations, but also other aspects of the archaeological work at Amarna. This photograph shows John D.S. Pendlebury and his collaborators, seated around a table at the entrance to the North Expedition House, preparing to pay the salaries of their Egyptian workmen.

Jean Capart, January 1934

Inv. EGI.09886

92. Boundary stelae, Amarna

a | b
c | d

The sacred territory of Amarna (Akhetaten), founded by Pharaoh Akhenaten, was marked by a series of boundary stelae carved into the cliffs surrounding the city on either side of the Nile. Sixteen such stelae are currently known. Stela U (a–b), flanked by statues of the pharaoh, his wife Nefertiti and two of their daughters, is located northeast of the city on the east bank of the Nile, while Stela A (c–d) occupies the west bank.

Jean Capart, 26 January 1930 (a–b), January 1934 (c), October–November 1945 (d)

Inv. EGI.07170 (a), EGI.07169 (b), EGI.09910 (c), EGI.012156 (d)

93. Landscape near Amarna

Two Egyptian men are washing clothes on the bank of the Nile in the region of Amarna, while a herd of cattle steps into the river to drink. A *saqiya* or traditional water-lifting device, driven by two bovids, is visible on the right. Further in the background, several *feluccas* are moored along the riverbank.

Ernest Orban-Viot, before 1909

Inv.EGI.05840

94. City and cemetery, Asyut

Strategically located in Middle Egypt, Asyut has been a bustling cosmopolitan city since pharaonic times. Today, it is one of Egypt's major cities and home to one of the largest communities of Coptic Christians. In 1930, Jean Capart photographed the expanding city's skyline, as well as the domed mausolea and tombs of its Muslim cemetery (in the foreground).

Jean Capart, 28 January or 17 March 1930

95. Queen Elisabeth of Belgium, Asyut

During the royal voyage of 1930, not only was Elisabeth, Queen of the Belgians, personally guided about by Jean Capart, but the Egyptian government also ensured that the queen visited sites and monuments in the most comfortable conditions possible. To climb to the top of the desert plateau overlooking the city of Asyut, she was carried in a sedan chair in the company of two Egyptian officials (each wearing a tarbush).

Jean Capart, 17 March 1930

Inv. EGI.07376

96. Mastaba K1, Beit Khallaf

Five large mudbrick mastabas dominate the low desert behind the village of Beit Khallaf. With its 2-metre-thick outer wall preserved to an astonishing height of 8 metres, mastaba K1 is the largest. These mastabas were excavated by John Garstang in 1901. Based on seal impressions bearing the royal name of Djoser that were found in tomb K1, they can be dated to the 3rd Dynasty. Garstang believed that K1 was the tomb of 3rd Dynasty Pharaoh Djoser.

Jean Capart, 30 January 1930

97. Mastaba K1, Beit Khallaf

One of the shafts of mastaba K1, leading to a stairway that gave access to the burial chamber located 25 metres below the surface. When Jean Capart photographed mastaba K1 in 1930, Garstang's identification of these mastabas at Beit Khallaf as royal tombs was still accepted. Today, however, they are considered private tombs contemporary to the 3rd Dynasty royal tombs at Saqqara in the north.

Jean Capart, 30 January 1930

Inv. EGI.07202

98. Crowds of Egyptians welcome Queen Elisabeth, Balliana

During the royal voyage of 1930, the yacht *Khassed Kheir*, placed at the disposal of Belgian Queen Elisabeth and her entourage by Egyptian King Fuad I, was welcomed throughout the country by enthusiastic crowds of people. Here, the dock at Balliana, near Abydos, is shown decked out with Egyptian and Belgian flags, as well as a banner wishing 'bonne arrivée' to the royal visitors.

Jean Capart, 19 March 1930

Inv. EGI.07503

99. Arrival of Queen Elisabeth, Balliana

Jean Capart photographed Elisabeth, Queen of the Belgians, on the deck of the yacht *Khassed Kheir* as she arrived at Balliana and was greeted by a crowd of Egyptians on the bank of the Nile. Later that day, they would visit the site of Abydos, with the magnificent Temple of Pharaoh Seti I.

Jean Capart, 19 March 1930

Inv. EGI.07488

100. Shunet el-Zebib, North Abydos

John Garstang, the director of the University of Liverpool expedition to Abydos in 1909, stands with a rifle in front of the niched exterior wall of the Shunet el-Zebib. This monumental mudbrick structure is the royal funerary enclosure built for Khasekhemwy, last king of the 2nd Dynasty, at Abydos. Originally the walls were covered entirely in a layer of white plaster, now largely disappeared but still visible at the base of the walls.

Jean Capart, 30 March 1909

Inv. EGI.01221

101. Middle Cemetery, North Abydos

The archaeological area known as the Middle Cemetery of North Abydos is located northwest of the Temple of Seti I. This large burial ground is home to the tombs of many important officials from the late Old Kingdom. In the background stands the excavation house of John Garstang and his team. In 1909, Jean Capart was invited to stay there while gathering data for his new book on the Temple of Seti I (published in 1912).

Jean Capart, 26 March–2 April 1909

Inv. EGI.01242

102. Excavation house, North Abydos

In 1907, John Garstang was granted permission to build this excavation house at Abydos. It stayed in use up until the 1950s, housing missions of the Egypt Exploration Fund/Society, which bought it from Garstang in 1909. After it fell into ruin, a new excavation house was constructed on the same spot in 1967 as a joint base for several American teams working at the site. Jean Capart photographed Garstang's original house in 1909. Note the recumbent jackal representing the god Wepwawet atop the roof's flag pole. This deity associated with mummification was particularly popular at Abydos.

Jean Capart, 26 March–2 April 1909

Inv. EGI.01230

103. House staff and workmen, North Abydos

Group photo of the house staff and some of the workmen from John Garstang's team near the excavation house.

Jean Capart (?), 26 March–2 April 1909

Inv. EGI.01229

104. Temple of Seti I, Abydos

The Temple of Seti I was one of Jean Capart's favourite monuments. During nearly each of his trips to Egypt, he visited this magnificent temple. In 1909, he even spent ten days at the site to photograph the temple for his book 'Abydos, le temple de Séti Ier'. This photograph shows part of the decoration for the north wall of the king's chapel with, from left to right, the god Thoth binding the *sema-tawy*, the goddess Seshat and Horus-Iunmutef.

Jean Capart (?), 31 December 1905 (?)

Inv. EGI.01006

105. Temple of Seti I, Abydos

The king's chapel in the Temple of Seti I is located behind the second hypostyle hall, together with six other chapels dedicated to different gods. Also on the north wall is another depiction of Iunmutef, here before an offering list. The Iunmutef priest is usually depicted wearing a leopard skin and a side lock of hair.

Jean Capart, 31 January 1930

106. Osireion, Abydos

Jean Capart poses with Éléonore Bille-de Mot and Marcelle Werbrouck (respectively sitting in the middle and to the right) and three other students, on top of an architrave block of the central hall of the Osireion, a cenotaph for the god Osiris. It was built in an archaic style, reminiscent of Old Kingdom temples. The Osireion is located at the rear of the Temple of Seti I, visible in the background.

Baudouin van de Walle, April 1925

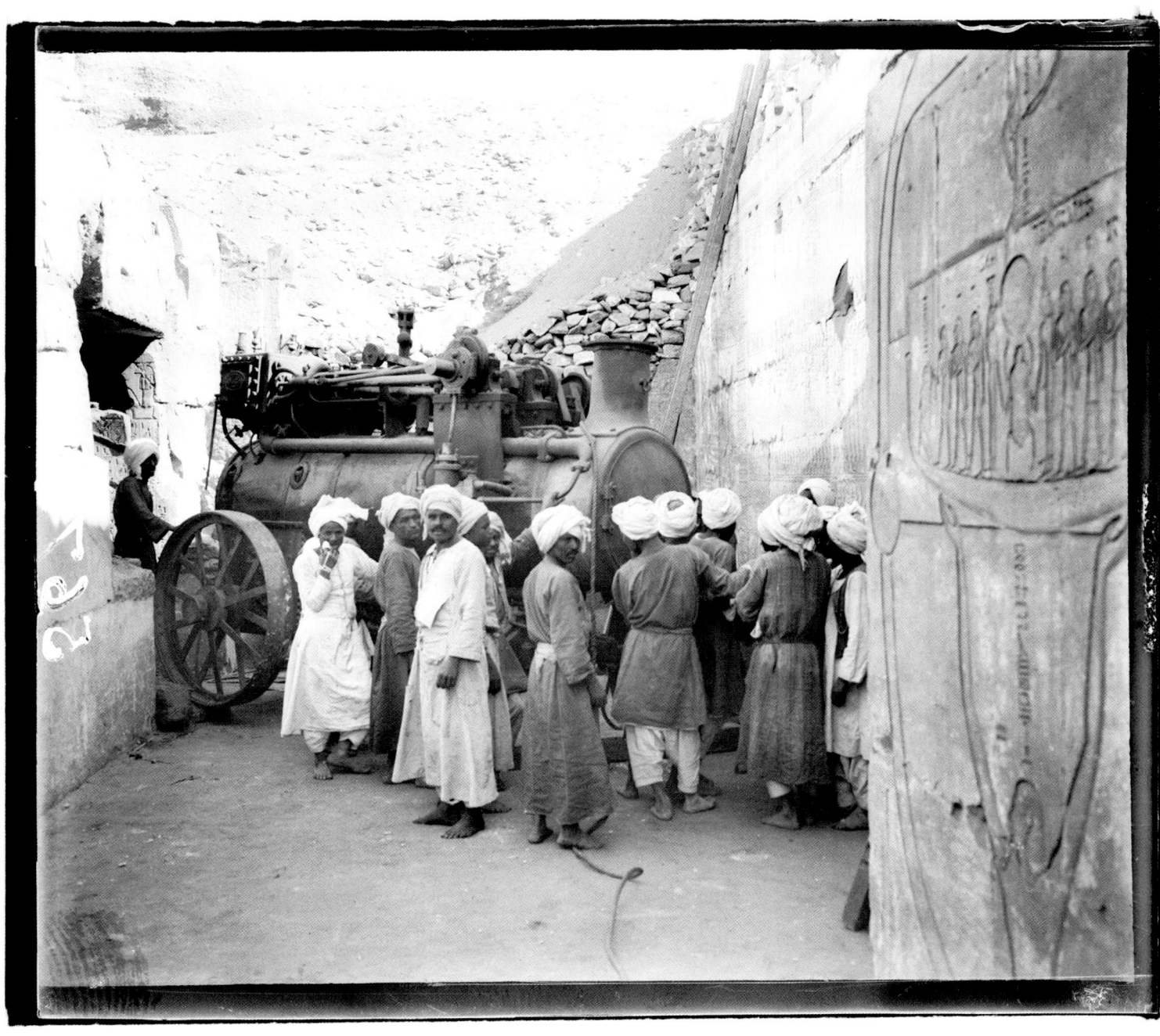

107. Osireion, Abydos

In 1925–1926, Baudouin van de Walle, a former student and close collaborator of Jean Capart, joined the team of Henri Frankfort, who then directed the excavations of the Egypt Exploration Society at Abydos. To evacuate the groundwater, Egyptian workmen are manoeuvring a steam engine and centrifugal pump with pipes, lent by Prince Yussef Kamel, through the Osireion's antechamber. Ironically, in the foreground, a relief can be seen that depicts the ancient Egyptian god Nun (the primordial waters) lifting up the boat of the rising sun, represented by a scarab beetle.

Baudouin van de Walle, 1926

108. Osireion, Abydos

The central hall of the Osireion was surrounded by a channel, accessed via two staircases at its eastern and western sides. The channel was originally filled with water directly from the Nile, but during the excavations, it was the rising groundwater that needed to be evacuated. This task fell to engineer Herbert Felton, here standing on a wooden beam, overlooking the eastern stairs of the central hall. A Western man wearing a hat (perhaps Henri Frankfort) is showing the work's progress to two unidentified Western women.

Baudouin van de Walle, 1926

Inv. EGI.05673

109. Osireion, Abydos

Long pipes were used to evacuate the water from the channel, which was then further cleared by the Egyptian workmen. Herbert Felton here supervises the pumping and clearing of the eastern section of the channel surrounding the Osireion's central hall. In the background, another Western man wearing a hat (perhaps Henri Frankfort) is watching the progress of the work.

Baudouin van de Walle, 1926

Inv. EGI.05674

110. *Fantasia*, Nag Hamadi

A large crowd has gathered on the banks of the Nile at Nag Hamadi, awaiting the arrival of the *Khassed Kheir*, the yacht of King Fuad I, carrying the Belgian Queen Elisabeth and Jean Capart. Musicians, horse riders and camel riders are getting ready to initiate a traditional *fantasia* in honour of the Queen.

Jean Capart, 20 March 1930

Inv. EGI.07485

111. Pigeon towers of Prince Yussef Kamel, Nag Hamadi

An Egyptian man walks amid a large flock of pigeons in the courtyard of Prince Yussef Kamel's pigeon tower complex at Nag Hamadi. This remarkable complex comprised no less than 45 towers, each containing nests for 15,000 pigeons. Jean Capart showed this place to Queen Elisabeth, later writing in his personal diary that this visit greatly amused the Queen.

Jean Capart, 20 March 1930

Inv. EGI.07372

112. Excavations at Tell Hiw

Workmen are walking on and off, emptying the subterranean galleries of a chapel in the ibis cemetery of Tell Hiw, excavated by Jean Capart and his team in 1927. Marcelle Werbrouck (seated in front of a dog), Marguerite Thirionet (standing to the right), an Egyptian man (standing to the left, Inspector Hakim Abu Seif?), and three other persons are posing upon the chapel's remains. The standing woman in black may be Claire Préaux.

Jean Capart, 14–20 February 1927

Inv. EGI.06101

113. Excavations at Tell Hiw

Jean Capart's wife Marguerite Thirionet also participated in the excavations at Tell Hiw, during her first ever trip to Egypt. This photograph shows her holding a falcon-headed bird mummy. Many such bird mummies were found within large ceramic jars deposited and buried within the subterranean galleries of the chapel of the Roman-period ibis cemetery.

Jean Capart, 14–20 February 1927

Inv. EGI.06113

114. Excavations at Tell Hiw

Detail of the relief decoration on the eastern wall of the easternmost room in the upper chapel of the Roman-period ibis cemetery. It shows the lower portion of a procession of Nile gods with flower bouquets. Atop the wall, the archaeologists have left a few of their finds: pottery vessels, oil lamps and a limestone block decorated in sunk relief.

Jean Capart, 14–20 February 1927

Inv. EGI.06106

115. Excavations at Tell Hiw

Fragment of a block decorated in sunk relief showing an offering to an Osirian ibis-headed god, photographed upside-down upon a table following its discovery.

Jean Capart, 14–20 February 1927

Inv. EGI.06103

116. Excavations at Tell Hiw

Local notables and several young boys visit the site to observe the excavations underway. The houses in the back belong to a small hamlet surrounding the nearby Coptic monastery, not far from the town of Hiw.

Jean Capart, 14–20 February 1927

117. Diospolis Parva, Tell Hiw

A group of villagers and two students of Jean Capart on a donkey gather at the foot of a large mound or *tell* with a domed building on top. This *tell* is most likely the ancient settlement of Diospolis Parva. The in-situ remains of a stone wall from a Greco-Roman temple are visible to the left, while in the foreground to the right, two Egyptian men and a boy are standing next to a wall built with inscribed blocks.

Jean Capart, April 1925

Inv. EGI.05242

118. Muslim cemetery, Tell Hiw

The tombs in the Muslim cemetery of Hiw are adorned with traditional painted decorations that may represent the funeral cloth that covered the coffin in which the deceased was carried to his or her final resting place. Such cloths also covered memorials placed on top of the graves. This cemetery is located south of the Roman-period fort of Diospolis Parva, which was excavated by William Matthew Flinders Petrie in 1898–1899.

Jean Capart, 14–20 February 1927

Inv. EGI.06235

119. *Shadufs*, Dendera

An unidentified Egyptian man, wearing a tarbush, stands on the bank of the Nile in front of a battery of *shadufs* in the area of Dendera. *Shadufs* were used since pharaonic times to lift water from the Nile and irrigate the agricultural land. They could be placed in a series, as seen here, if the water needed to be elevated to a much higher level. The *shaduf* is sometimes still used today in the more rural parts of the Nile Valley, though it is being replaced by water pumps.

Jean Capart, January–February 1934

Inv. EGI.09801

120. *Fantasia*, Dendera

A blind singer, supported by a large crowd, welcomes Queen Elisabeth of Belgium and Jean Capart at Dendera. The Queen and Capart visited the Temple of Dendera a few days after attending the official opening of the burial chamber of Tutankhamun. To travel to Dendera, they used a boat placed at their disposal by Abd el-Aziz Yahia Bey, the governor of Qena.

Jean Capart, 22 February 1923

Inv. EGI.00779

121. Temple of Hathor, Dendera

A group of musicians greets Queen Elisabeth of Belgium and Jean Capart at the Temple of Hathor in Dendera. They are standing in front of a Roman-period fountain located just outside the temple's northern propylon gateway. A curious crowd has gathered on the archaeological mounds to observe the spectacle.

Jean Capart, 22 February 1923

Inv. EGI.00860

122. Village of Naqada

Together with Hierakonpolis and Abydos, Naqada was one of ancient Egypt's earliest important urban centres. It gave its name to the Naqada Culture of Predynastic Egypt (4th millennium BCE) that initially manifested itself in Upper Egypt, before gradually spreading to the entire country. Little now remains of the vast cemeteries and settlements once present in the area, and Naqada has become a modest rural community on the west bank of the Nile.

Jean Capart, 3 February 1930

Inv. EGI.07232

123. 'Royal Tomb', Naqada

One of Naqada's most important monuments is a large mudbrick mastaba with a niched facade, discovered and excavated in 1896 by Jacques de Morgan. Its attribution to Menes, Egypt's legendary first pharaoh, caused much debate, and current views suggest that it actually belonged to Neith-Hotep, wife of Aha, second king of the 1st Dynasty. This photograph by Jean Capart is a rare image of this monument today built over by a mosque.

Jean Capart, 3 February 1930

Inv. EGI.07235

124. Temple of Montu, Medamud

With ropes and wooden rollers, workmen remove a large reused lintel block from the foundations of the Temple of Montu at Medamud, while Ferdinand Bisson de la Roque of the Institut Français d'Archéologie Orientale observes the operation. The block was found beneath the doorway of Amenhotep II and the western wall of the temple's pronaos. The lintel originally belonged to a monument erected in honour of the *heb-sed* festival of Middle Kingdom Pharaoh Senusret III.

Jean Capart, January–March 1929

Inv. EGI.04009

125. Carter House, Luxor

During his exploration of the Valley of the Kings, Howard Carter lived in this domed mudbrick house, located on Luxor's west bank near the valley entrance. After completing his excavation of the tomb of Tutankhamun, Carter retired from archaeological work, but continued to reside here during the winter. Preserved and recently restored, this heritage house today welcomes visitors.

Jean Capart, 16 February–13 March 1923

Inv. EGI.00498

126. Tomb of Tutankhamun (KV62), Valley of the Kings

After the discovery of Tutankhamun's tomb in November 1922, its burial chamber was officially opened on 18 February 1923 in the presence of several Egyptian and foreign high officials, including Queen Elisabeth of Belgium and her son Crown Prince Leopold. The resultant media frenzy was unprecedented and Jean Capart, who accompanied the Queen, photographed part of the international press present at the event.

Jean Capart, 18 February 1923

Inv. EGI.00790

127. Tomb of Tutankhamun (KV62), Valley of the Kings

By late February 1923, Carter and his team were in need of a break and he temporarily closed the tomb of Tutankhamun. Egyptian workmen and children covered the tomb entrance with debris in order to protect it. This operation lasted several days and was photographed by Jean Capart.

Jean Capart, 28 February 1923

Inv. EGI.00772

128. Temple of Hathor, Deir el-Medina

In 1921, Bernard Bruyère of the Institut Français d'Archéologie Orientale began his excavations at Deir el-Medina. This ancient village on the west bank of Luxor had been home to the workmen and artisans who had built and decorated the New Kingdom royal tombs in the Valley of the Kings and the Valley of the Queens. This photograph shows Marguerite Thirionet (standing) and Marcelle Werbrouck before the later Ptolemaic Temple of Hathor at Deir el-Medina.

Jean Capart, January–March 1929

Inv. EGI.07509

129. Temple of Hathor, Deir el-Medina

The Ptolemaic Temple of Hathor testifies to the continued use of the Deir el-Medina site after the New Kingdom. This rare photograph of a young Jean Capart was taken inside the temple, probably by his student Charles Mathien. Capart sits upon a pronaos wall decorated with scenes depicting Ptolemy VI worshipping different gods.

Charles Mathien (?), 29 December 1905

Inv. EGI.00900

130. Mortuary Temple of Seti I, Qurna

The west bank of Thebes, modern Luxor, was the burial ground of the pharaohs and their entourage during the New Kingdom. Several mortuary temples, named 'Houses of Millions of Years' in ancient Egyptian, were constructed at the edge of the Theban desert for the cult of the deceased kings. This photograph shows Charles Mathien standing in front of the sun altar in the solar court of the Mortuary Temple of Pharaoh Seti I.

Jean Capart, 28 December 1905

Inv. EGI.00872

131. Expedition camp, Deir el-Bahari

The design of the Mortuary Temple of Hatshepsut, visible in the background, was based on that of 11th Dynasty King Mentuhotep II, located just next to it. They were both excavated by a team of the Egypt Exploration Fund, directed by Édouard Naville. Jean Capart visited the site and camp of the mission in 1905. In his notebook, he describes how he was guided around by Charles T. Currelly, a member of the British mission.

Jean Capart, 26 December 1905

Inv. EGI.00890

132. Mortuary Temple of Hatshepsut, Deir el-Bahari

The Mortuary Temple of Queen Hatshepsut, with its remarkable design of colonnaded terraces, was built against the cliffs of the natural amphitheatre at Deir el-Bahari. Located on the west bank of the Nile, it lies almost directly opposite the east-bank Temple of Amun. This photograph well conveys its dramatic landscape setting.

Jean Capart, 11 or 14 February 1946

Inv. EGI.12136

133. Mortuary Temple of Hatshepsut, Deir el-Bahari

The upper-terrace pillars of the Temple of Queen Hatshepsut support colossal statues of the queen depicted as Osiris. When Jean Capart visited the site in 1946, they were being restored by a team of the Service des Antiquités de l'Égypte, directed by Émile Baraize. The granite doorway, visible behind the pillars, leads to the upper court or festival courtyard and the axial sanctuary of the temple.

Jean Capart, 11 or 14 February 1946

Inv. EGI.12140

134. Mortuary Temple of Hatshepsut, Deir el-Bahari

Fragment of a column bearing the Horus name of Pharaoh Thutmose II, located on the third terrace of the Mortuary Temple of Queen Hatshepsut. Several such columns lined the court of the upper terrace, and this one originally would have stood almost 5 metres tall.

Jean Capart, 17 November 1945

Inv. EGI.12142

135. Mortuary Temple of Hatshepsut, Deir el-Bahari

Detail of the raised-relief decoration on the northern wall of the chapel of Hatshepsut, within the queen's mortuary temple at Deir el-Bahari. This was one of two chapels in the Royal Cult Complex located on the temple's upper terrace. It shows rows of offering bearers bringing provisions for the queen, and is considered one of the finest examples of a royal offering scene from ancient Egypt.

Jean Capart, January–February 1934

Inv. EGI.09962

136. Mortuary Temple of Hatshepsut, Deir el-Bahari

This photograph taken by Aram Alban shows Jean Capart seated upon the southern parapet of the ramp leading up to the second terrace of the Temple of Hatshepsut. A sitting lion in sunk relief adorns this part of the ramp. This portrait was taken during Capart's final trip to Egypt in 1946, and is probably one of the last photographs that exist of him in Egypt.

Aram Alban, 14 February 1946

Inv. EGI.12370 (reproduction of a photographic print)

137. Mummy seller, Deir el-Bahari

A young Egyptian boy holds up the head of a pharaonic mummy that he tries to sell at Deir el-Bahari. Mummies, or parts thereof, were often sold to tourists already in the 19th century, both as collectable antiquities and to be ground into powder for their perceived medicinal properties.

Photographer unknown, no date but probably 1909

Inv. EGI.01226

138. Mortuary Temple of Ramesses II, Luxor

The Mortuary Temple of Ramesses II, called the Ramesseum, is seen here from the hills of Sheikh Abd el-Qurna on the Theban west bank. In the background, on the right, the Colossi of Memnon tower above the cultivated plain extending from the Nile and modern Luxor, visible on the horizon. High officials from the royal court built their tombs at Sheikh Abd el-Qurna overlooking the various New Kingdom mortuary temples. The modern houses in the foreground were constructed on top of and in between these private tombs.

Jean Capart, 27 or 28 December 1905

139. Mortuary Temple of Ramesses II, Luxor

Three students of Jean Capart stand on the roof slabs of the central aisle of the hypostyle hall of the Ramesseum, the Mortuary Temple of Ramesses II. The colossal Osirian pillar of the king (in the foreground) belongs to the second court, located in front of the hypostyle hall. Next to the pillar, an unidentified photographer is setting up his camera and tripod.

Jean Capart, April 1925

Inv. EGI.05328

140. Mortuary Temple of Amenhotep III, Kom el-Hetan

Queen Elisabeth of Belgium stands next to the northern Colossus of Memnon, one of the twin statues representing Pharaoh Amenhotep III erected in front of the first pylon of his mortuary temple at Kom el-Hetan. The statues' name derives from their Roman-period inscriptions in Greek and Latin, particularly on the northern one, that repeatedly mention the name Memnon, the Homeric king of Ethiopia who defended Troy.

Jean Capart, 14–16 March 1923

Inv. EGI.05366

141. Mortuary Temple of Amenhotep III, Kom el-Hetan

Large inscribed fragments of quartzite are strewn about the fields at Kom el-Hetan. They belong to the northern stela that once stood in the peristyle court of what was the largest mortuary temple ever built in the Theban necropolis. Together with its southern counterpart, both stelae recount the achievements of Amenhotep III and have since been reconstructed at their original location within the temple.

Jean Capart, 14 November 1945

Inv. EGI.12151

142. Mortuary Temple of Ramesses III, Medinet Habu

Since 1924, the Mortuary Temple of Ramesses III at Medinet Habu on the Theban west bank has been studied by the Epigraphic Survey of the University of Chicago Oriental Institute. To systematically record and copy the high temple walls, they employed a hanging seat secured to the top of the temple. An epigrapher of the Oriental Institute is here seen hanging against the northern tower of the first temple pylon, holding an epigraphic drawing on his lap. The ropes are controlled below by a group of Egyptian workmen.

Jean Capart, 22 March 1930

Inv. EGI.07388

143. Mortuary Temple of Ramesses III, Medinet Habu

During her visit of Medinet Habu in 1930, Belgian Queen Elisabeth insisted on experiencing firsthand the hanging seat used by the American epigraphers. She is here seen smiling as she scales the northern tower of the first temple pylon. In his personal diary, Jean Capart wrote that the Queen said that 'she felt like a fly on these gigantic figures'.

Jean Capart, 22 March 1930

Inv. EGI.07384

144. Mortuary Temple of Ramesses III, Medinet Habu

Together with her entourage, Queen Elisabeth of Belgium (to the far left, with a white umbrella) admires the decoration of the northern exterior wall of the Mortuary Temple of Ramesses III at Medinet Habu. Belgian politician and royal physician Pierre Nolf (third from the left) carries the queen's personal camera and stands next to Countess Ghislaine de Caraman-Chimay, the queen's lady-in-waiting.

Jean Capart, 22 March 1930

145. Mortuary Temple of Ramesses III, Medinet Habu

Jean Capart stands between the remains of the ruined mudbrick buildings in the northern section of the temple complex, as he looks through the lens of his Bellieni stereoscopic camera. The background shows excavations overseen by Uvo Hölscher, who cleared this area of the site.

Paul Polinet, 22 March 1930

Inv. EGI.07469 (reproduction of a photographic print)

146. Small Temple, Medinet Habu

In the late 19th century, fragments of a colossal statue representing Amenhotep III, his wife Tiye and three of their daughters were discovered near the Mortuary Temple of Ay/Horemheb at Medinet Habu. In 1897, Georges Daressy moved the fragments to the court of the Small Temple in front of the Mortuary Temple of Ramesses III, where Jean Capart photographed them in 1905. This photograph shows the royal face of Pharaoh Amenhotep III.

Jean Capart, 27 or 29 December 1905

Inv. EGI.01002

147. Small Temple, Medinet Habu

Fragment of the colossal statue of Amenhotep III and his wife Tiye, here seen wearing a vulture headdress. Between 1906 and 1908, the fragments of this statue were moved to the Egyptian Museum in Cairo, where they were restored and reassembled by a team directed by Alexandre Barsanti and Max Fanghaenel. This statue is still the centrepiece of the Egyptian Museum's atrium (JE 33906 + M610) and constitutes the largest family group statue ever found in Egypt.

Jean Capart, 27 or 29 December 1905

Inv. EGI.01003

148. Great Temple of Amun, Karnak

An unidentified Western man walks down the dromos of the Amun Temple at Karnak, lined on either side with a row of ram-headed sphinxes. To the south lies the Decauville railway that was used to evacuate debris from the excavations inside the temple. It runs in front of the house of Georges Legrain (to the left), the French Egyptologist who investigated the site of Karnak for almost 25 years.

Jean Capart, probably 1909

Inv. EGI.01320

149. Great Temple of Amun, Karnak

View from atop the first pylon of the Temple of Amun, showing the forecourt with the second pylon, the columns of the kiosk of Taharqa and the bark shrine of Ramesses III. The eighth and ninth pylons are visible in the background.

Jean Capart, 16 February–13 March 1923

Inv. EGI.00416

150. Great Temple of Amun, Karnak

An Egyptian man unfolds a mat that covered a decorated block of the Red Chapel of Hatshepsut (block 33 in the numbering system of Pierre Lacau and Henri Chevrier). This block was stored with many others north of the temple forecourt, which was used by Georges Legrain for sorting reused blocks found throughout the complex. In the background, an unidentified Western woman, probably a student of Jean Capart, sits in the shade.

Jean Capart, April 1925

Inv. EGI.05196

151. Great Temple of Amun, Karnak

Built with small stone blocks (known as *talatat*), the temples of Pharaoh Akhenaten became a convenient source of building material after his death. His successors dismantled them and reused the *talatat* for the construction of new temples. In the Amun Temple at Karnak, Georges Legrain and his team found large quantities of *talatat* in the foundations of the great hypostyle hall and the ninth pylon. They were piled up in a storage yard south of the temple's great court built around 1895–1896 by the Service des Antiquités de l'Égypte, where Capart photographed them in 1925.

Jean Capart, April 1925

152. Great Temple of Amun, Karnak

A group of four men and a dog clamber amongst collapsed blocks in the southern portion of the great hypostyle hall of the Temple of Amun at Karnak. The man with the pith helmet is probably Georges Legrain. He is in the company of British Egyptologist Henry R.H. Hall (behind Legrain), Sydney P. Hall (in front) and Charles Mathien. The accumulation of big blocks and column drums are a mix of the collapsed remains of the second pylon's southern tower and the hypostyle hall's southern rows of columns.

Jean Capart, 24 December 1905

Inv. EGI.00917

153. Great Temple of Amun, Karnak

Since 1895, Georges Legrain (in the centre, wearing a pith helmet) and his team had striven to consolidate and rebuild the great hypostyle hall of the Temple of Amun. This photograph recalls the delicate operation of removing a 50-ton architrave block from the southern portion of the hypostyle hall. Note the flags and palm branches attached to the block by the workmen to bless this operation.

Jean Capart, 21 April 1909

Inv. EGI.01518

154. Great Temple of Amun, Karnak

After the death of Georges Legrain in 1917, his work was continued by the French architect Maurice Pillet.
Under the latter's supervision, the stabilisation works in the southern portion of the great hypostyle hall continued.
This photograph shows the wooden struts placed between columns 13 and 14.

Jean Capart, April 1925

Inv. EGI.05148

155. Great Temple of Amun, Karnak

As was common in temples of the New Kingdom, obelisks were also erected in front of several pylons at the Karnak Temple. This photograph shows the lower part of the northern obelisk of Queen Hatshepsut in the court of the fourth pylon. The red granite obelisk's inscription mentions that its carving took seven months of labour.

Jean Capart, January–March 1938

156. Great Temple of Amun, Karnak

In 1897, Georges Legrain found several fragments of a colossal quartzite statue of Amun, including the head, bust and right leg pictured here. The statue dates to the reign of Tutankhamun (later usurped by Horemheb), with the god displaying the facial features of the young king. The fragments were found in the antechamber of the bark sanctuary and moved by Legrain to the doorway to the northern court of the sixth pylon, where they were photographed by Jean Capart. A fragment of the nose of this same statue was recovered in 2003.

Jean Capart, 20–21 April 1909

Inv. EGI.01345

157. Great Temple of Amun, Karnak

In 1905, Jean Capart witnessed firsthand the excavations carried out by Georges Legrain and his team. This photograph shows a group of Egyptian workers moving a heavy object (an architectural block or a statue fragment?) out of the excavation area in the court between the seventh and eighth pylons of the Karnak Temple. The object is hung from a wooden pole carried on their shoulders. The striding colossi in the background flanking the seventh pylon represent Pharaoh Thutmose III.

Jean Capart, 24 December 1905

Inv. EGI.00925

158. Great Temple of Amun, Karnak

In 1937, one of the worksites of the French team in Karnak, then under the direction of Henri Chevrier, was the court between the eighth and ninth pylons of the Amun Temple. Shown here is the facade of the eighth pylon, originally built by Queen Hatshepsut, with several colossal statues representing different pharaohs. The best preserved one (on the left) depicts Amenhotep I. In the courtyard, Egyptian workmen are moving a large block from the excavation area using ropes and wooden rollers.

Jean Capart, February 1937

Inv. EGI.05108

159. Great Temple of Amun, Karnak

Four students of Jean Capart have climbed the colossal statue of a seated pharaoh representing Amenhotep I in front of the eighth pylon of the Amun Temple at Karnak. Two of them can be identified as Baudouin van de Walle (standing on the right arm of the statue) and Éléonore Bille-de Mot (seated in the middle).

Jean Capart, April 1925

Inv. EGI.05157

160. Great Temple of Amun, Karnak

In the court of the eighth pylon of the Amun Temple, Egyptian workers are excavating the area around the base of an obelisk. Egyptian boys, carrying baskets on their heads, walk on and off to remove the debris. The pylon's western tower is visible in the background, as well as a Decauville railway in front of it. On the horizon emerge the mudbrick houses of the modern village of Karnak.

Jean Capart, 24 December 1905

Inv. EGI.00924

161. Great Temple of Amun, Karnak

Ceremonial gateways or pylons were an essential architectural feature in Egyptian temples from the Middle Kingdom onwards. Their two tapering towers could symbolise the *akhet*, the place on the horizon where the sun rises between two mountains. The Great Temple of Amun at Karnak has no less than ten pylons, underlining the importance of this temple. This photograph shows the remains of the western tower of the ninth pylon.

Jean Capart, 20–21 April 1909

162. Bucheum, Armant

Like the sacred Apis bulls buried in the Serapeum at Saqqara, their southern counterparts, the Buchis bulls, were also interred in a complex of underground catacombs, known as the Bucheum at Armant. When Jean Capart visited the site in 1930, the excavations directed by Robert L. Mond on behalf of the Egypt Exploration Society had just exposed tombs 11 and 12 and one of the large sandstone sarcophagi in which sacred bulls had been buried.

Jean Capart, 8 February 1930

Inv. EGI.07248

163. King Albert I and Queen Elisabeth, Armant

Although Capart wrote in his personal diary after his visit to Armant in February 1930 that the place was 'located at the end of the world' and 'infested with snarling dogs', he returned there just a few weeks later with the Belgian royal couple, King Albert I (the tall man in the centre) and Queen Elisabeth (in white to his right). They were personally guided around the site by Robert L. Mond (behind the Queen, to the right) and were here photographed on their way to the Bucheum.

Jean Capart, 26 March 1930

Inv. EGI.07407

164. Temple of Montu, Tod

When Jean Capart photographed the Temple of Montu at Tod in 1934, a French mission directed by Fernand Bisson de la Roque was conducting its first excavation season at the site. Two Western women stand within the first vestibule of the Ptolemaic pronaos, while two Western men are climbing the stairs to the upper storeroom. Two years later, in 1936, a large collection of silver objects, now known as the Tod Treasure, was found in four chests below the Middle Kingdom temple, in its foundations.

Jean Capart, January–February 1934

Inv. EGI.09950

165. Village of Tod

When the French mission started working at the site, large parts of the Temple of Montu were built over by modern houses and many architectural remains were reused by the villagers. This decorated architrave block was recarved and used as a trough in the courtyard of a village house. However, some scholars have suggested that this block originally belonged to the Temple of Montu at Armant, located on the opposite bank of the Nile.

Jean Capart, January–February 1934

Inv. EGI.09946

166. Step pyramid, el-Kula

In 1945, Jean Capart obtained permission to excavate the small enigmatic step pyramid at el-Kula. On 9 November 1945, a team of 61 workmen supervised by *reis* (foreman) Chared Mohammed Mansur and Arpag Mekhitarian, started excavations at the site. As is the case for the six other similar pyramids known from different sites throughout the Nile Valley, no burial chamber was found at the pyramid of el-Kula. Generally considered to date to the 3rd Dynasty, the exact function of these seven small step pyramids remains uncertain, but they were clearly not intended as burial places. This photograph shows the clearance of the north side of the pyramid.

Jean Capart, 19 November 1945

Inv. EGI.12157

167. The 'Fort', Hierakonpolis

Like the Shunet el-Zebib at Abydos, this monumental mudbrick enclosure was built by King Khasekhemwy of the 2nd Dynasty. Although dubbed the 'Fort', it had no military function, but also differs in many ways from the funerary enclosures at Abydos. It is currently believed to have been built in commemoration of Khasekhemwy's rejuvenation festival or even Egypt's reunification under his reign.

Jean Capart, no date but probably 1937

Inv. EGI.11374

168. Village of el-Mahamid

The village of el-Mahamid is located a few kilometres north of Elkab, the site where Jean Capart started excavating in 1937. From Luxor, Capart and his team travelled to Elkab by train. They were awaited at the station of el-Mahamid by some of Capart's Egyptian collaborators, continuing on to Elkab by donkey. This photograph shows the southern edge of the village, today one of the largest villages in the Elkab area.

Jean Capart, 1938

Inv. EGI.11491

169. Town wall, Elkab

In 1905, Jean Capart passed by Elkab for the first time, the site that would become so important in his career. From the train, he took this photograph of the northern corner of the town's massive mudbrick wall, the so-called Great Wall of Elkab. It would take him 25 years to actually visit the place and another seven years to start excavations at the site. Note the steam clouds of the locomotive floating past the lens of Capart's camera.

Jean Capart, 21–23 December 1905

Inv. EGI.00875

170. Town wall, Elkab

In the company of the American Goldman family, Jean Capart set foot within the Great Wall of Elkab for the very first time and fell in love with the site. Symbolically, this happened on Valentine's Day 1930. Impressed by this visit, he added Elkab to the programme of the royal voyage, so returning a few weeks later on 27 March. There, he declared to Queen Elisabeth of Belgium that 'if one day we have the means, it is here that I would like to work!'

Jean Capart, 14 February 1930

Inv. EGI.07268

171. Start of the excavations at Elkab

On 16 February 1937, Jean Capart kicked off the very first excavation season at Elkab. At 8 am, 35 Egyptian workmen, led by *reis* Chared Mohammed Mansur, gathered at the south side of the temple enclosure and started excavations within the temple complex. This photograph was taken during this first day of excavations and marks the beginning of Belgian archaeological research at Elkab, which continues to this day.

Jean Capart, 16 February 1937

Inv. EGI.11343

172. The Quftis, *reis* Chared and his three sons, Elkab

During his three seasons of fieldwork at Elkab, Jean Capart could count on specialised labourers from the town of Quft, known as Quftis. These men had built up great expertise in excavation since the late 19th century and worked at sites all over Egypt. At Elkab, they were supervised by reis Chared Mohammed Mansur, who is here pictured in the centre of the group of twenty Quftis, wearing a white galabiya. His three sons Anwar, Sayf and Kamal are seated in front.

Jean Capart, 6 February 1946 (?)

Inv. EGI.12234

173. The workmen at Elkab

Apart from the Quftis, Jean Capart and his team also employed a number of local workmen from the nearby villages of el-Mahamid, Hilal and el-Nasrab. These workmen earned lower wages than the Quftis and were engaged in less specialised labour, such as hauling away dirt and moving stone blocks. This photograph shows the large group of workmen within the enclosure wall of Elkab at the end of the 1937 season.

Jean Stiénon, 16 February–24 March 1937

Inv. EGI.11411 (reproduction of a photographic print)

174. The *ghafir* Mahmud, Elkab

Besides the Quftis and local workmen, various other people worked at the Elkab site. One of them was the guard (*ghafir* in Arabic) Mahmud Ahmed Ali, already there when Jean Capart had first visited Elkab back in 1930 with Belgian Queen Elisabeth. Mahmud well remembered that earlier visit when Capart actually started work at the site in 1937. The *ghafirs* were employed by the Egyptian Antiquities Service to guard the site.

Jean Capart, 9 November–31 December 1945

Inv. EGI.12187

Mohammed at Elkab in March 2012

175. Nabawiya and Mohammed, Elkab

The youngest daughter and son of *ghafir* Mahmud, Nabawiya and Mohammed, were regular visitors to the excavation site. Mohammed, who was seven or eight years old when this photograph was taken, later worked for many seasons with the Belgian mission at Elkab, as would some of his sons. Two of his grandsons also followed in his footsteps and have been part of the Elkab team for over fifteen years. Mohammed died peacefully at Elkab in 2015.

Éléonore Bille-de Mot, 16 February–24 March 1937

Inv. EGI.11207 (reproduction of a photographic print) + Photograph of Mohammed, son of *ghafir* Mahmud, Elkab, 12 March 2012 (© Belgian archaeological Mission to Elkab)

176. Excavations at Elkab

The site of Elkab harbours many temples, both within the town enclosure and out in the desert hinterland. The main temple was dedicated to Elkab's principal deity, the vulture goddess Nekhbet, who was also the tutelary goddess for the whole of Upper Egypt. A smaller temple was built up against the Temple of Nekhbet and dedicated to the god Thoth. This photograph shows the clearance of the latter temple's northern outer wall.

Jean Capart, March 1937

Inv. EGI.11428

177. Excavations at Elkab

The lower part of a naophorous statue and a granite head were found east of Temple B, located in front of the first pylon of the Temple of Nekhbet. The head displays royal regalia, such as the *nemes*, *uraeus* and false beard, and was identified by Jean Capart as Pharaoh Hakor (Akoris) of the 29th Dynasty. The naophorous statue represents Wesirwer, mayor of Thebes, scribe and priest of Montu. Both objects are now in the Egyptian Museum, Cairo (JE 89121 & JE 89124).

Jean Capart, 27 February 1937

Inv. EGI.11215

178. Excavations at Elkab

The extant remains of the main temples at Elkab primarily date to the Ramesside (19th Dynasty) and Late Period (7th–4th century BCE), but older blocks belonging to previous building phases of the temple were reused. This photograph shows a decorated block bearing the cartouche of Thutmose III of the 18th Dynasty, integrated upside down into the eastern outer wall of the Temple of Nekhbet.

Jean Capart, 17–19 February 1938

Inv. EGI.11494

179. Excavations at Elkab

Older phases of the temple were also recognised. Decorated blocks found in the court in front of the second pylon of the Temple of Nekhbet were identified as belonging to a bark shrine erected by the 13th Dynasty King Sobekhotep III. Even older blocks were unearthed at other places within the temple complex of Elkab. This photograph shows a decorated block, bearing the cartouche of Pharaoh Mentuhotep III of the 11th Dynasty, right after it was unearthed below one of the sanctuaries of the Temple of Thoth.

Jean Capart, 27 February 1938

180. Excavations at Elkab

Workmen are removing a large ceiling slab from crypt B in the Temple of Nekhbet, with its famous mythological scene depicting the seven speeches of Nekhbet. Under the supervision of Jean Stiénon (right), *reis* Chared Mohammed Mansur (to the left, with his arms in the air) encourages the workmen and sets the rhythm to which the heavy stone is hauled away. The curved mudbrick construction in front of the Great Wall is part of the Old Kingdom enclosure wall of the town of Elkab.

Jean Capart, 3 March 1938

Inv. EGI.11477

181. Excavations at Elkab

The mythological scene depicting the seven speeches of Nekhbet is located on the western wall of her temple's crypt. After the crypt was opened, the principal scene was copied by the French Egyptologist and artist Marcelle Baud. Loose blocks, such as the one in this photograph, were found during the crypt's excavation and complement the scene on the western wall.

Jean Capart, 12–20 February 1938

Inv. EGI.9627

182. Excavations at Elkab

A young man sits on the remains of the northern wall of the eastern sanctuary of the Temple of Thoth. Here again, decorated blocks were reused to close the underground crypt and as foundations for the sanctuary pavement. The cartouche visible here, bears the name of Pharaoh Thutmose III.

Jean Capart, 19 February 1938

Inv. EGI.11556

183. The Elkab team at the site in 1937

During the first excavation season at Elkab, the Belgian contingent of Jean Capart's team consisted of collaborators and colleagues from the museum, supplemented by a young architect recommended to Capart by the famous Art Nouveau architect Victor Horta, a colleague of his at the Belgian Royal Academy. Capart has here photographed the team, with from left to right: Arpag Mekhitarian, architect Jean Stiénon, Violette Verhoogen, Éléonore Bille-de Mot and Marcelle Werbrouck.

Jean Capart, 16 February–24 March 1937

Inv. EGI.11434

184. Somers Clarke House, el-Nasrab

The two men pictured here in front of the Somers Clarke House—the excavation house of the Belgian mission—were members of the house staff. On the left is Badri, son of Sheikh Ibrahim, a guardian and messenger. On the right is Abd el-Baghi, also named Abdu, who was a *sufragi* from Luxor. The Somers Clarke House, or 'Beit Clarke' as it is called in Arabic, is a conspicuous landmark and well-known throughout the wider Elkab region. It was built in 1906 by Somers Clarke, a British archaeologist, who was one of the first to excavate at Elkab.

Jean Capart, 9 November–31 December 1945

Inv. EGI.12164

185. Somers Clarke House, el-Nasrab

Somers Clarke was also an architect and constructed and restored train stations, churches and other buildings in Egypt. Adherent to the Arts and Crafts movement, he followed traditional Egyptian building techniques and applied these principles to the construction of his own mudbrick house at el-Nasrab, located a few kilometres south of Elkab. Clarke died in 1926 and was buried next to his house. In 1937, it became the base of operations for Jean Capart and the Belgian mission, and has remained so ever since. Note the Belgian and old Egyptian flags flying on Beit Clarke's roof terrace.

Jean Capart, 17 January–16 March 1938

Inv. EGI.11666

186. The Elkab team in 1937, el-Nasrab

This group photo of the Elkab team was taken on the northern terrace of Beit Clarke on 21 February 1937, the very day that Capart celebrated his 60th birthday. The Quftis and *reis* Chared Mohammed Mansur are all dressed up for the occasion and stand in the back, while the Belgian team members are seated in the front. From left to right: Jean Stiénon, Éléonore Bille-de Mot, Marcelle Werbrouck, Violette Verhoogen and Arpag Mekhitarian.

Éléonore Bille-de Mot, 21 February 1937

Inv. EGI.11296 (reproduction of a photographic print)

187. *Fantasia* at Somers Clarke House, el-Nasrab

To celebrate Jean Capart's 60th birthday, a *fantasia* was organised by the workmen in his honour. The usual *tahtib* (an Upper Egyptian stick-fighting folk dance) was followed by a belly dance performance in the courtyard in front of Beit Clarke, which Capart captured in this photograph. Apart from the workmen, a few women from the neighbourhood also attended the *fantasia* and can be seen in the background. According to Capart, they were mainly interested in catching a glimpse of his female collaborators Marcelle Werbrouck, Éléonore Bille-de Mot and Violette Verhoogen.

Jean Capart, 21 February 1937

Inv. EGI.11344

188. Sheikh Qusi, el-Nasrab

Atop one of the hills in front of Beit Clarke stands the tomb of Sheikh Qusi. It is no longer known who he was, but sheikhs were important people, widely respected, and venerated for different reasons. Sheikh tombs are usually painted turquoise blue, the typical colour so prevalent in traditional Muslim architecture. At the national holiday festival of Sham el-Nessim, the local villagers gather around these tombs to picnic.

Jean Capart, 16 February–24 March 1937

Inv. EGI.11224

189. *Saqiya*, Edfu

Two cows led by a young farmer set the horizontal toothed wheel of a *saqiya* in motion. This photograph was taken by Jean Capart during the royal voyage of 1923, when Queen Elisabeth of Belgium and Capart made several visits and excursions outside Luxor after attending the official opening of the burial chamber of the tomb of Tutankhamun. To the left, an Egyptian army officer of the Queen's escort is attending the demonstration.

Jean Capart, 5 March 1923

Inv. EGI.00906

190. The Nile steamer *Fostat*, Gebel Silsila

For their Nile cruise in 1930, the American Goldman family and Jean Capart travelled in the sternwheel steamer *Fostat* of the company Thomas Cook & Son. The boat was photographed here at the quarry site of Gebel Silsila. Besides Capart, many Egyptologists have made use of the *Fostat*. In the 1960s, it was sold to the Oriental Institute (University of Chicago) and served as a floating excavation house during the Nubian rescue campaign. Later, the *Fostat* was moored at the Giza Bridge in Cairo, where it was turned into the residence of the director of the American Research Center in Egypt.

Jean Capart, 15 February 1930

Inv. EGI.07314

191. Sandstone quarries, Gebel Silsila

The day after Jean Capart and the Goldman family visited Elkab, the *Fostat* moored at the site of Gebel Silsila West, where they visited the rock Temple of Horemheb and other rock-cut shrines, as well as the spectacular sandstone quarries exploited for the construction of so many ancient Egyptian monuments. This photograph shows Bernhard Gutmann and perhaps Marguerite Thirionet in the central area of the quarries.

Jean Capart, 15 February 1930

Inv. EGI.07308

192. Temple of Sobek and Haroeris, Kom Ombo

The Temple of Kom Ombo was one of the main centres where the crocodile god Sobek was worshipped. Temples dedicated to Sobek usually had a pool for crocodiles, who were considered sacred, and were mummified and buried in cemeteries around the temple. Baudouin van de Walle photographed these two *ghafirs* before the Chapel of Hathor, south of the main temple, carrying a newly discovered crocodile mummy. All in all, more than 300 crocodile mummies were found in the vicinity of the temple.

Baudouin van de Walle, 1926

193. Tomb of Harkhuf, Qubbet el-Hawa

An Egyptian man sits in the entrance to the tomb of Harkhuf at Qubbet el-Hawa on the west bank of Aswan. Harkhuf was an Overseer of Upper Egypt during the 6th Dynasty. His tomb's facade, partly pictured here, was decorated with an autobiographical text in which Harkhuf recounts four expeditions to Nubia by order of Kings Merenre and Pepi II. This text gives important insights into Egypt's relations with Nubia at the end of the Old Kingdom, but Harkhuf's greatest achievement seems to have been, on his last expedition, his bringing a dwarf back to Egypt for King Pepi II.

Baudouin van de Walle, 1926

194. Unfinished obelisk, Aswan

Early in the morning of 16 February 1930, the steamer *Fostat* moored at Aswan, where Jean Capart and the Goldman family would spend two entire days exploring different sites in the area. That afternoon, they went with two cars to the granite quarry with the unfinished obelisk. This would have been the largest obelisk ever erected in ancient Egypt, had it not broken while still in the quarry. A long crack can be seen running through its top.

Jean Capart, 16 February 1930

Inv. EGI.07323

195. Ancient granite quarries, Aswan

Marguerite Thirionet poses beside an unfinished Roman-period bathtub, somewhere in the area of Aswan's southern quarries. The large granite boulders behind are natural formations of the landscape.

Jean Capart, 17 February 1930

Inv. EGI.07326

196. Temple of Isis, Philae

Ever since the construction of the Aswan Low Dam in 1902, the Temple of Isis on the island of Philae was regularly flooded. The temple was then only accessible by boat, as this Egyptian man demonstrates. This photograph shows, from left to right, the rear wall of the eastern colonnade, as well as the first and second pylons of the temple. Jean Capart took a particular interest in this temple. At his request, a scale model of the island and the temple was made and exhibited in the Egyptian rooms of the museum. For the museum archives, he also acquired many of the almost 1,600 photographs of the temple made by the Prussian Academy of Sciences in Berlin in 1908–1909 and 1909–1910.

Jean Capart, 22 December 1905

Inv. EGI.00910

197. Kiosk of Trajan, Philae

A large portion of the temple complex at Philae was built during the Ptolemaic period, but important changes and additions to the site were made in Roman times. A good example is the well-known kiosk of Trajan, located east of the Isis Temple, and here photographed by Capart following the annual flood in 1905.

Jean Capart, 22 December 1905

Inv. EGI.07008

198. Queen Elisabeth of Belgium at Philae

Queen Elisabeth of Belgium and her entourage visited the flooded Temple of Isis in 1930. They are seen here on the roof of the temple, which is almost completely submerged. The temple was moved to the higher nearby island of Agilkia as part of the UNESCO Nubian rescue campaign in the 1960s, and the building is no longer flooded.

Jean Capart, 30 March 1930

Inv. EGI.07380

199. Fortified town, Qasr Ibrim

Two Egyptian men and two members of the American Goldman family stand in front of Temple 1 at the site of Qasr Ibrim. After the Aswan High Dam's completion in 1970, Qasr Ibrim was one of the few archaeological sites south of the dam not to be submerged by the waters of Lake Nasser. Contrary to other monuments and temples relocated during the UNESCO Nubian rescue campaign, the site still stands in its original position, now forming an island in the southern part of Lake Nasser.

Jean Capart, 19 February 1930

Inv. EGI.07337

200. Temple of Ramesses II, Abu Simbel

Of all the monuments relocated during the UNESCO Nubian rescue campaign, the rock-cut Temple of Ramesses II at Abu Simbel is probably the most famous. In 1930, Jean Capart visited the temple then still at its original location, and took this photograph of the facade with its four seated colossi of Ramesses II. Much to Capart's dismay, Egyptian technicians were at that very moment installing an electric lighting system (bottom left). His frustration is clearly recorded in his personal travel diary of 1930.

Jean Capart, 19 February 1930

201. Middle Kingdom fortress, Semna

His Nile cruise with the Goldman family brought Jean Capart as far south as the Second Cataract. From Wadi Halfa, they drove by car to Semna, the southernmost of a series of Egyptian fortresses built during the Middle Kingdom in Lower Nubia. This photograph shows the remains of houses and a temple inside the eastern fortress of the site, with the ruins of the western fortress visible in the background. From his personal travel diary, we know that this visit made a great impression on Capart.

Jean Capart, 20 February 1930

Inv. EGI.07354

Glossary[1]

Abd el-Baghi (Abdu) (dates unknown)   No. 184
Head *sufragi* in the team of Jean Capart during the excavations at Elkab. He was from Luxor and was recommended to Capart by French colleagues.

Abd el-Latif Salem (dates unknown)   No. 13-14, 23
One of the overseers of the workmen during the excavations of Jean Capart at Heliopolis in 1907.

Abd el-Rahim (dates unknown)   No. 28-29, 40
Egyptian man who is frequently mentioned in the notes of Jean Capart as early as 1909. He lived at the village of Nazlet el-Samman in Giza, where Capart and his wife would visit him regularly. He introduced Capart to several antiquities dealers in Cairo.

Abdallah (dates unknown)   No. 17, 20, 23
Sufragi in the team of Jean Capart during the excavations at Heliopolis in 1907.

Abd el-Aziz Yahia Bey (dates unknown)   No. 120
Governor of Qena in Upper Egypt. He lent his boat to Queen Elisabeth of Belgium and Jean Capart during the royal voyage of 1923.

Aha (c. 3000 BCE)   No. 123
Second king of the 1st Dynasty. He moved the central administration of the incipient pharaonic state from southern Egypt to the new capital of Memphis. Although he was still buried in the royal necropolis of Umm el-Qaab at Abydos, the first elite mastaba tombs were constructed during his reign at the Memphite necropolis of Saqqara.

Ahmed Fakhry (1905-1973)   No. 40
Egyptian archaeologist. He studied at Cairo University, but completed his Egyptological training abroad, including in Brussels with Jean Capart. He is mainly known for his work in the desert oases, but also excavated at Giza with Selim Hassan.

Akhenaten (1352-1336 BCE)   No. 92, 151
Tenth king of the 18th Dynasty. Originally named Amenhotep IV, he changed his name to Akhenaten when he established the cult of the Aten (sun disc) and built a new capital at Amarna.

Akhet   No. 161
Egyptian hieroglyph representing the two mountains of the horizon between which the sun rises.

Alban, Aram (1883-1961)   No. 136
Armenian-Egyptian photographer who lived and worked in Egypt, Belgium and France. Apart from his work as an art photographer, he also portrayed European and Egyptian nobility. Royals such as Queen Elisabeth of Belgium were part of his clientele, as well. He made several portraits of Jean Capart in 1945–1946.

Albert I (1875-1934)   No. 163
King of Belgium (r. 1909–1934). He married the Bavarian Duchess Elisabeth in 1900. After their official state visit to Egypt and King Fuad I in 1930, Elisabeth made a Nile cruise with Jean Capart as her guide while Albert visited Iraq. He joined the cruise for a few days during visits in Luxor and Armant.

Amenemhat III (1831-1786 BCE)   No. 63, 72-73
Sixth king of the 12th Dynasty. He was buried in his pyramid complex at Dahshur, but also built a second funerary complex at Hawara in the Fayum. He was important for the Fayum's development by enlarging the Bahr Yussef, and he erected two colossal statues of himself at Biahmu.

Amenhotep I (1525-1504 BCE)   No. 158-159
Second king of the 18th Dynasty. Under his reign, the workmen's village of Deir el-Medina was founded, but the location of his tomb remains uncertain.

Amenhotep II (1427-1400 BCE)   No. 124
Seventh king of the 18th Dynasty. Contrary to his father Thutmose III who invested considerably in the expansion of the Temple of Amun at Karnak, he focused more on smaller temples. His name is recorded at several sites, such as Medamud, Tod, Armant, Qasr Ibrim and Semna.

Amenhotep III (1390-1352 BCE)   No. 140-141, 146-147
Ninth king of the 18th Dynasty. Under his reign, artistic tradition reached a pinnacle, and of no other pharaoh have more statues survived. His mortuary temple at Kom el-Hetan was the largest ever built in the Theban necropolis.

Amun   No. 3, 82, 132, 148-161
One of the principal gods in the Egyptian pantheon, who was worshipped in temples across Egypt and Nubia. During the New Kingdom, he became the chief deity, often merged with the sun god Re into Amun-Re, and his temples at Karnak and Luxor were of national importance.

---

[1] The date ranges given for kings of ancient Egypt are their regnal years, while the date ranges for modern people are the years of their birth and death.

Ange Abela (dates unknown)   No. 21-22

Dragoman or interpreter in the team of Jean Capart during the excavations at Heliopolis in 1907.

Anubis   No. 124

God of the Egyptian underworld and death, associated with the afterlife and mummification. He is usually represented as a canine or a man with a canine head.

Apis bull   No. 49, 162

Sacred bull that was worshipped in the Temple of Ptah at Memphis. Apis bulls were embalmed after their death and buried in large sarcophagi in the underground catacombs of the Serapeum at Saqqara.

Ay (1327-1323 BCE)   No. 146

Penultimate king of the 18th Dynasty and successor to Tutankhamun. He continued the religious reforms of his predecessor after the Amarna period. He built a mortuary temple at Medinet Habu, usurped by his successor Horemheb.

Ayer, Edward Everett (1841-1927)   No. 58

American businessman and early benefactor of the Field Museum of Natural History in Chicago. He primarily collected books and manuscripts on native American history, but also acquired Egyptian antiquities.

Badri Ibrahim (dates unknown)   No. 184

Son of Sheikh Ibrahim who lived in the village of el-Nasrab. He worked as a guard, messenger and boatman in the team of Jean Capart during the excavations at Elkab.

Baraize, Émile (1874-1952)   No. 33-34, 133

French architect who initially worked for the Egyptian railways, but later became the assistant of Alexandre Barsanti, whom he succeed as Director of Works at the Service des Antiquités de l'Égypte in 1912. He excavated and restored many sites in Egypt, including the Great Sphinx at Giza and the Temple of Hatshepsut at Deir el-Bahari.

Barsanti, Alexandre (1858-1917)   No. 43, 147

Italian architect and Egyptologist at the Service des Antiquités de l'Égypte. He worked and excavated at many sites in Egypt and Nubia, including the Mortuary Temple of Ramesses III at Medinet Habu (as assistant to Georges Daressy) and the North Pyramid at Zawiyat el-Aryan.

Baud, Marcelle (1890-1987)   No. 90, 181

French artist and Egyptologist. She was the first female Egyptologist to enter the Institut Français d'Archéologie Orientale in Cairo (1921). Through her friendship with Marcelle Werbrouck, she also became a close collaborator of Jean Capart and participated in the excavations at Elkab in 1938.

Belzoni, Giovanni Battista (1778-1823)   No. 65

Italian excavator and explorer who dug at many sites in Egypt and Nubia in search of antiquities for Henry Salt, the British Consul-General in Egypt.

Bille-de Mot, Éléonore (1903-1987)   No. 2, 106, 159, 175, 183, 186-187

Belgian Egyptologist. She was the daughter of Jean Capart's friend and colleague Jean De Mot. After the death of her father in the Battle of Passchendaele during World War I, Capart took her under his wing. She studied with Capart and became one of Belgium's first female Egyptologists. In 1937, she participated in the first excavation season at Elkab.

Bisson de la Roque, Ferdinand (1885-1958)   No. 124, 164

French Egyptologist at the Institut Français d'Archéologie Orientale and later the Musée du Louvre. In 1937, he visited Jean Capart at Elkab and helped him with logistical matters. The Decauville railways used by Capart at Elkab were lent to him and brought over from the site of Tod.

Boghos Nubar Pasha (1851-1930)   No. 8

Son of former prime minister of Egypt, Nubar Pasha. He was an entrepreneur, banker and corporate officer in several companies. He partnered with Édouard Empain to create the new suburb of Heliopolis.

Borchardt, Ludwig (1863-1938)   No. 46

German Egyptologist and architect who was the first director of the Deutsches Archäologisches Institut in Cairo. After his retirement in 1929, he founded the Ludwig Borchardt Institute, which in 1940 became the Schweizerische Institut für Ägyptische Bauforschung und Altertumskunde in Cairo. He worked at many sites, including Philae, Abu Ghurab, Abusir and Amarna.

Breccia, Evaristo (1876-1967)   No. 2

Italian archaeologist. After working with several Italian missions in Egypt, in 1904 he became director of the Greco-Roman museum in Alexandria, where he remained until 1931 when he was appointed professor at the University of Pisa.

Bruyère, Bernard (1879-1971)   No. 128

French Egyptologist at the Institut Français d'Archéologie Orientale in Cairo. He worked for more than thirty years at the site of Deir el-Medina.

Buchis bull   No. 162

Sacred bull and southern counterpart of the Apis bull. They were interred in sandstone sarcophagi in the underground catacombs of the Bucheum at Armant.

Campbell, Patrick (1779-1857)   No. 41

Scottish diplomat and army officer, who was appointed as Consul-General in Egypt in 1833. One of the chambers in the Pyramid of Khufu, as well as tomb LG 84/G 9500 at Giza were named after him by their discoverer Howard Vyse.

Capart, Jean (1877-1947)   All photos, except 7, 31, 33, 55, 57, 60-61, 93, 108-109, 137, 175, 192-193

Belgian Egyptologist and first curator of the Egyptian collection at the Royal Museums of Art and History in Brussels. Held the first chair in Egyptology at the University of Liège, directed the first Belgian excavations in Egypt, and was the founder of the Fondation (now Association) Égyptologique Reine Élisabeth. For all of this, he is considered the founder of Belgian Egyptology.

Carter, Howard (1874-1939)   No. 125, 127

British Egyptologist who discovered the tomb of Tutankhamun in 1922. As an excavator and draughtsman, he worked at different sites in Egypt from 1891 onwards. After a dispute with tourists at Saqqara in 1905, he resigned from his position at the Service des Antiquités de l'Égypte. With the support of Lord Carnarvon, in 1909 he started excavations in the Valley of the Kings, where he would find five other royal tombs prior to his discovery of the tomb of Tutankhamun.

Chared Mohammed Mansur (unknown-1970)   No. 166, 171-172, 180, 186

Reis in the team of Jean Capart during the excavations at Elkab. He was recommended to Capart by American colleagues. After Capart's death in 1947, he continued to work as a *reis* for the Belgian mission. He died on 18 June 1970 and is buried in his hometown of Quft.

Chevrier, Henri (1897-1974)   No. 150, 158

French architect who succeed Maurice Pillet as Director of Works for the Service des Antiquités de l'Égypte at Karnak.

Clarke, Somers (1841-1926)   No. 184-188

British architect and archaeologist who moved to Egypt in 1902. Besides his architectural work, he was one of the first archaeologists to explore the region of Elkab at the end of the 19th century and also excavated there between 1901 and 1904. In 1937, his personal house at Elkab became the Belgian excavation house and has remained so ever since.

Cleopatra VII (69-30 BCE)   No. 5

Queen during the Ptolemaic Period between 51–30 BCE and last ruler of the dynasty. The obelisks referred to as Cleopatra's Needles were made for her and now stand in New York's Central Park and on the Victoria Embankment in London.

Couyat-Barthoux, Jules (1881-1965)   No. 15

French geologist and archaeologist, and member of the Service de la Carte géologique de France. He worked in Egypt and Morocco, before joining the Délégation archéologique française to Afghanistan in 1925.

Coxe, Eckley Brinton (1872-1916)   No. 69

American philanthropist and prominent benefactor of the Egypt Exploration Fund. He sponsored several excavations in Egypt and Nubia, including the work of the University Museum of Pennsylvania, directed by Alan Rowe, at the site of Meidum.

Cumont, Franz (1868-1947)   No. 42-43, 48-49

Belgian archaeologist and historian. He was a professor at Ghent University and curator at the Royal Museums of Art and History in Brussels until 1912. A cofounder of the Academia Belgica in Rome (1939), he was also the first archaeologist to work at the site of Dura Europos in Syria.

Currelly, Charles Trick (1876-1957)   No. 131

Canadian Egyptologist who was curator and director of the Royal Ontario Museum, and professor at the University of Toronto. For the Egypt Exploration Fund, he worked at many sites in Egypt, including Deir el-Bahari.

Daressy, Georges (1864-1938)   No. 146

French Egyptologist who was assistant keeper of the Bulaq Museum in 1887. He was in charge of the transfer of the Egyptian collections from Bulaq to Giza (1891) and later to the Egyptian Museum (1902). Also in 1891, he was one of the excavators of the more than 250 coffins of the priests of Amun found in the Second Cache of Deir el-Bahari. Ten of these coffins are now part of the Egyptian collection in Brussels.

de Caraman-Chimay, Ghislaine (1865-1955)   No. 144

Belgian aristocrat, countess and lady-in-waiting to Queen Elisabeth of Belgium. She accompanied the Queen in Egypt during the royal voyage of 1930.

de Morgan, Jacques (1857-1924)   No. 123

French archaeologist and prehistorian who was director-general of the Service des Antiquités de l'Égypte between 1892 and 1897. He worked at many sites in Egypt, such as Naqada, Dahshur and Saqqara, where he discovered the mastaba of Mereruka. He is considered a founder of the study of Egyptian prehistory.

Deutsche Orient-Gesellschaft (1898-today)   No. 46

German research organisation, founded in 1898, that promotes interest and research in the archaeology of the Near East. Since 1902, the DOG has organised excavations in Iraq, Palestine, Israel, Turkey and Syria. In Egypt, excavations have been carried out at the sites of Abusir, Abusir el-Meleq and Amarna.

Diocletian (284-305)   No. 2

Roman emperor. The large monolithic column in Alexandria known as Pompey's Pillar originally supported a 7-metre-tall porphyry statue of him.

Djedefre (2566-2558 BCE)   **No. 24**
Fourth king of the 4th Dynasty. He was Khufu's son and successor, but built his own pyramid complex at Abu Rawash.

Djehutihotep (c. 1850 BCE)   **No. 86**
Last nomarch or governor of the 15th Upper Egyptian nome, who lived during the 12th Dynasty and was buried at Deir el-Bersha.

Djoser (2667-2648 BCE)   **No. 47-48, 54-55, 59, 62, 96**
Second king of the 3rd Dynasty. His step pyramid at Saqqara was the first pyramidal funerary complex ever built and also the first royal monument constructed entirely of stone.

Egypt Exploration Fund/Society (1882-today)
     No. 88-90, 102, 107, 131, 162
British organisation founded in 1882 to promote archaeological and Egyptological research in Egypt. Immediately following the First World War, in 1919, its name was changed to the Egypt Exploration Society. Many institutions, both British and foreign, supported its excavations financially and received in exchange vast allotments of the excavated objects. Jean Capart and the Royal Museums of Art and History were an important benefactor of this partage model that considerably enriched the Egyptian collection in Brussels.

Elisabeth of Bavaria (1876-1965)   **No. 69, 79, 95, 98-99, 110-111, 119-120, 126, 140, 143-144, 163, 170, 174, 189, 198**
Duchess of Bavaria and Queen of Belgium (r. 1909–1934). As a patroness of the arts, she gave her name to the Queen Elisabeth Competition for classical music, as well as to the Fondation (now Association) Égyptologique Reine Élisabeth, created by Jean Capart in 1923 following their visit to the official opening of the burial chamber of the tomb of Tutankhamun.

Empain, Édouard (1852-1929)   **No. 6, 8, 11, 57**
Belgian entrepreneur, banker and industrialist who was a benefactor of the Royal Museums of Art and History and its Egyptian collection in particular. He financed the acquisition of the mastaba of Neferirtenef, as well as asking Capart to excavate in Heliopolis where he was to build an entire new suburb.

Fantasia   **No. 110, 120, 187**
Traditional spectacle with horsemanship performances. More generally, it also designates a party or fun festival involving music and dance.

Felton, Herbert (1888-1968)   **No. 108-109**
British engineer and photographer who worked at the Osireion at Abydos between 1925 and 1927. He was also a commercial photographer specialised in architecture. In 1941, he was the first photographer employed by the National Buildings Record (now part of the Historic England Archive), which collected photos of monuments and sites at risk during and after World War II.

Firth, Cecil Mallaby (1878-1931)   **No. 54-55**
British Egyptologist who was a member of the Service des Antiquités de l'Égypte for over 30 years. Most of his career was spent at Saqqara, where he excavated the pyramid complex of Teti, but also and more importantly the step pyramid complex of Djoser.

Frankfort, Henry (1897-1954)   **No. 107-109**
Dutch Egyptologist. He studied and worked with William Matthew Flinders Petrie and directed excavations for the Egypt Exploration Society at Amarna, Abydos and Armant.

Fuad I (1868-1936)   **No. 79, 98, 110**
Seventh son of Khedive Ismail. He was sultan of Egypt and Sudan in 1917, and crowned king of Egypt and Sudan in 1922. He was also a 'high protector' of the Fondation (now Association) Égyptologique Reine Élisabeth.

Galabiya   **No. 172**
Traditional Egyptian garment.

Garstang, John (1876-1956)   **No. 96-97, 100-103**
British archaeologist and founder of the Liverpool Institute of Archaeology. He excavated at many sites in Egypt and Nubia, including Beit Khallaf, Naqada, Abydos and Hierakonpolis. In 1909, he welcomed Jean Capart for almost ten days at his dig house in Abydos. The Royal Museums of Art and History were an important benefactor of Garstang's excavations, particularly in Nubia and Abydos.

Ghafir   **No. 85, 174-175, 192**
Arabic word for guard. *Ghafirs* were recruited by the Service des Antiquités de l'Égypte and by excavation teams to guard their sites, but also the missions' excavation houses.

Goldman, Julius (1852-1938)   **No. 81**
American lawyer and oldest son of Marcus Goldman, founder of the investment bank Goldman Sachs. Through his son-in-law Ashton Sanborn, who was an archaeologist and secretary at the Museum of Fine Arts in Boston, Julius and his family became close friends with Jean Capart. With Capart as their guide, the Goldman family made a cruise on the Nile in 1930.

Gunn, Battiscombe George (1883-1950)   **No. 55**
British Egyptologist who excavated for the Egypt Exploration Society at Amarna, and at Saqqara on behalf of the Service des Antiquités de l'Égypte. Before becoming professor of Egyptology at Oxford, he was appointed curator between 1931 and 1934 at the Philadelphia University Museum, where he also met Capart who in the 1930s regularly visited the USA in his capacity as advisory curator at the Brooklyn Museum.

Gutmann, Bernhard (1869-1936)   No. 81, 191
German-American painter who was married to Bertha Goldman, the youngest daughter of Julius Goldman. They both joined the 1930 Nile cruise, which inspired a few of Gutmann's paintings.

Hakim Abu Seif (dates unknown)   No. 112
Egyptian inspector for the Service des Antiquités de l'Égypte. He was assigned to supervise the excavations led by Jean Capart at Tell Hiw in 1927.

Hakor (393-380 BCE)   No. 177
Second king of the 29th Dynasty, also known as Akoris. His name is found in different parts of the Temple of Nekhbet at Elkab. The head of a statue, identified by Jean Capart as representing Hakor, was also found there. It is now kept in the Egyptian Museum in Cairo (JE 89124).

Hall, Henry Reginald Holland (1873-1930)   No. 152
British Egyptologist and keeper of Egyptian and Assyrian antiquities at the British Museum. He participated in excavations at Deir el-Bahari and Abydos, as well as at important sites in Mesopotamia, such as Ur.

Hall, Sydney Prior (1842-1922)   No. 152
British portrait painter and illustrator, and father of British Egyptologist Henry R.H. Hall.

Harkhuf (c. 2280 BCE)   No. 193
Overseer of Upper Egypt during the reigns of Pharaohs Merenre and Pepi II of the 6th Dynasty. The autobiographical text on the facade of his tomb at Qubbet el-Hawa is the oldest narrative of foreign travel known from ancient Egypt.

Hathor   No. 121, 128-129, 192
One of the principal goddesses in the Egyptian pantheon. She is often depicted as a cow and considered the divine mother of the reigning king.

Hatshepsut (1473-1458 BCE)   No. 131-136, 150, 155, 158
Sixth ruler of the 18th Dynasty. She was the second historically confirmed female pharaoh and one of Egypt's most prolific builders, as illustrated by her mortuary temple at Deir el-Bahari.

Heb-sed   No. 124
Renewal and regeneration ritual celebrated by the king after a reign of 30 years.

Herishef   No. 76-77
Fertility god depicted in the form of a ram or a ram-headed man. His principal temple was located at Ihnasiya el-Medina.

Hölscher, Uvo (1878-1963)   No. 145
German archaeologist and architect. He worked with Ludwig Borchardt and the Deutsches Archäologisches Institut at Abusir, Giza and Amarna, before joining the Oriental Institute mission at Medinet Habu, where he directed the excavations in the Mortuary Temple of Ramesses III between 1926 and 1937.

Horemheb (1323-1295 BCE)   No. 146, 156, 191
Last king of the 18th Dynasty. He was a general under Pharaoh Tutankhamun and succeeded Ay to the throne. He restabilised the country after the tumultuous Amarna period and had the Aten Temples at Amarna dismantled.

Horta, Victor (1861-1947)   No. 183
Belgian architect and designer. He was one of the founders and leading figures of the Art Nouveau movement. He was a colleague of Jean Capart at the Belgian Royal Academy, and upon his recommendation the young architect Jean Stiénon joined the excavations at Elkab in 1937 and 1938.

Horus   No. 104, 134
Falcon-god who was the pharaoh's protector and the embodiment of divine kingship. He is one of the earliest Egyptian deities and attested to since the Early Dynastic period.

Ibrahim (dates unknown)   No. 184
Egyptian sheikh who lived in the village of el-Nasrab. His sons Ahmed and Badri worked in the team of Jean Capart during the excavations at Elkab.

Institut Français d'Archéologie Orientale (1880-today)   No. 124, 128
French research institute in Cairo, founded in 1880. Many of Egypt's most important and well-known sites, such as Deir el-Medina and Karnak, have been investigated by archaeologists and Egyptologists attached to the institute.

Isis   No. 196-198
Important goddess of ancient Egypt. As the mother of Horus, she is also the symbolic mother of the king. Her cult spread beyond the borders of Egypt during the Greco-Roman period.

Ismail Salem (dates unknown)   No. 13
Egyptian workman in the team of Jean Capart during the excavations at Heliopolis in 1907. His precise function is not known.

Iunmutef   No. 104-105
A complex concept, Iunmutef, which literally means 'Pillar of his Mother', was a divine priest usually depicted wearing a leopard skin and a side lock of hair. With functions comparable to those of Horus as heir to the throne, he was linked to kingship and the maintenance of cosmic order.

Jéquier, Gustave (1868-1946)   **No. 63**
Swiss Egyptologist who spent a large part of his career excavating different pyramid complexes at Saqqara. He held the first chair of Egyptology at the University of Neuchâtel.

Junker, Herman (1877-1962)   **No. 35**
German Egyptologist, professor of Egyptology at the Universities of Vienna and Cairo, and director of the Deutsches Archäologisches Institut. He carried out ground-breaking work at many sites in Egypt and Nubia, particularly in Giza, where he systematically cleared a large part of the mastaba fields between 1912 and 1929.

Khafre (2558-2532 BCE)   **No. 32, 34, 44**
Fourth king of the 4th Dynasty. He was the son of Khufu and succeeded his half-brother Djedefre. He built the second pyramid at Giza, and the face of the Great Sphinx, placed in front of his pyramid, is thought to represent him.

Khasekhemwy (2610-2593 BCE)   **No. 100, 167**
Last king of the 2nd Dynasty. He was the most prolific builder of the Early Dynastic period, as illustrated by his monumental tomb and its accompanying Shunet el-Zebib funerary enclosure (both located at Abydos), as well as the so-called 'Fort' at Hierakonpolis.

Kheir Aballah (dates unknown)   **No. 72**
Local inhabitant of Biahmu in the Fayum.

Khentkawes I (c. 2500 BCE)   **No. 34, 38-39**
Female ruler at the end of the 4th and beginning of the 5th Dynasties. She was buried in a remarkable tomb, close to the pyramid complex of Menkaure on the Giza Plateau.

Khufu (2589-2566 BCE)   **No. 29-31, 34-38, 40, 44**
Second king of the 4th Dynasty and builder of the Great Pyramid at Giza. Many quarrying and mining expeditions were organised during his reign and an inscription bearing his name was also found in the desert hinterland south of Elkab.

Lacau, Pierre (1873-1963)   **No. 150**
French Egyptologist who in 1912 was appointed director of the Institut Français d'Archéologie Orientale, before serving from 1914 to 1936 as head of the Service des Antiquités de l'Égypte. In this capacity, he oversaw the work of many archaeological missions, including the excavations of Jean Capart at Tell Hiw in 1927, as well as the clearance of the tomb of Tutankhamun. He strongly advocated for all objects of this tomb to remain in Egypt and succeeded in retaining them for the Egyptian Museum in Cairo.

Legrain, Georges (1865-1917)   **No. 148, 150-154, 156-157**
French Egyptologist and member of the Institut Français d'Archéologie Orientale. Almost his entire career was dedicated to the excavation and restoration of the Temple of Amun at Karnak on behalf of the Service des Antiquités de l'Égypte. Since they first met at Karnak in December 1900, a long-lasting friendship developed between Legrain and Jean Capart.

Leopold III (1901-1983)   **No. 126**
Oldest son of King Albert I and Queen Elisabeth of Belgium, and fourth king of Belgium (r. 1934–1951). He was still crown prince when he joined his mother and Jean Capart at the official opening of the burial chamber of the tomb of Tutankhamun on 18 February 1923.

Lepsius, Karl Richard (1810-1884)   **No. 27**
German Egyptologist who greatly expanded our knowledge of the hieroglyphic system. He was professor of Egyptology at the University of Berlin and co-director of the Egyptian Museum in Berlin. He led the Prussian expedition to Egypt and Sudan (1842–1845), modelled after the Napoleonic mission, which resulted in the multivolume *Denkmäler aus Ägypten und Äthiopien*. This expedition spent several months in the Memphite necropolis, documenting the pyramid sites of Giza, Abusir, Saqqara and Dahshur.

Mackay, Ernest (1880-1943)   **No. 66**
British archaeologist. During the first part of his career, he worked at different sites in Egypt. After the First World War, he continued his research in the Near East. From 1935 onwards, he shifted his focus to the archaeology of the Indus Valley.

Mahmud Ahmed Ali (dates unknown)   **No. 174-175**
Ghafir at Elkab when Jean Capart and his team excavated there. He was already based at Elkab when Queen Elisabeth of Belgium and Jean Capart had earlier visited the site in 1930.

Marcel, Alexandre (1860-1928)   **No. 11**
French architect who created a Japanese pagoda for the Tour du Monde attraction at the Paris World Fair of 1900. It was bought by King Leopold II of Belgium, who had it reconstructed on the grounds of the Royal Palace in Laeken (Brussels). For Édouard Empain's urban project at Heliopolis, he developed the French Quarter, as well as his private residence.

Mariette, Auguste (1821-1881)   **No. 48-49, 59**
French Egyptologist, founder of the Service des Antiquités de l'Égypte (1858) and the Egyptian Museum in Bulaq (1863). A leading figure in the development of modern Egyptology, his discovery of the Serapeum at Saqqara was one of his greatest achievements.

Mathien, Charles (1855-1935)
  No. 7, 12, 14, 20-21, 23, 32, 42-45, 48, 58-59, 129-130, 152
Belgian physician who studied Egyptology under Jean Capart at the University of Liège. He joined Capart during his mission at Saqqara in 1905 (mastaba of Neferirtenef) and the excavations at Heliopolis in 1907.

Mayence, Fernand (1879-1959)   No. 12, 20

Belgian archaeologist and professor at the Université Catholique de Louvain. He excavated with Jean Capart at Heliopolis in 1907 and became his colleague at the Royal Museums of Art and History, where he was appointed curator in 1922. He also directed the excavations for the Brussels museum at the site of Apamea in Syria.

Mekhitarian, Arpag (1911-2004)   No. 166, 183, 186

Belgian Egyptologist of Armenian descent who was born in Egypt. He studied under Jean Capart and became one of his closest collaborators. In 1930, he joined Capart for part of the Nile cruise with the American Goldman family, as well as the subsequent royal voyage. He also participated in the excavation seasons at Elkab. From 1947 until 1994, he was the secretary-general of the Fondation (now Association) Égyptologique Reine Élisabeth.

Memnon   No. 138, 140

Greek mythological king of Ethiopia who came with his army to the defence of Troy. His name was lent to the two colossal statues of Amenhotep III at his mortuary temple at Kom el-Hetan: the Colossi of Memnon.

Menes (c. 3000 BCE)   No. 123

Legendary first king and founder of the unified Egyptian state. Whether Menes is to be identified with the historical figures Narmer or Aha is still debated. Current views seem to support an identification of Menes as Narmer.

Menkaure (2532-2503 BCE)   No. 37-38, 44

Fifth king of the 4th Dynasty and builder of the third pyramid at Giza. Several triad statues were found in the valley temple of his pyramid complex; showing the king with several deities, they are considered among the finest examples of Old Kingdom sculpture.

Mentuhotep II (2055-2004 BCE)   No. 131

Sixth king of the 11th Dynasty. He reunified Egypt after the tumultuous First Intermediate Period by overthrowing the Herakleopolitan rulers. He installed Egypt's capital in Thebes, where he also built a terraced mortuary temple, after which Queen Hatshepsut later modelled hers.

Mentuhotep III (2004-1992 BCE)   No. 179

Seventh king of the 11th Dynasty. Blocks bearing his name were found in the Temple of Nekhbet at Elkab.

Merenptah (1213-1203 BCE)   No. 64

Fourth king of the 19th Dynasty. Few monuments built during his reign still survive, a notable exception being his palace, located next to the Temple of Ptah at Kom el-Qala in Memphis.

Merenre (2287-2278 BCE)   No. 193

Fourth king of the 6th Dynasty. He sent trade expeditions to Lower Nubia, which were commemorated in stelae found in the Aswan area, as well as in the autobiographical text of Harkhuf.

Mereruka (c. 2350 BCE)   No. 51

High official of the early 6th Dynasty. He was vizier, chief justice, and inspector of the priests of the Pyramid of Teti. His tomb at Saqqara lies near that of his father-in-law, King Teti.

Mohammed Mahmud Ahmed (unknown-2015)   No. 175

Son of *ghafir* Mahmud Ahmed Ali. He was a young boy when Jean Capart and his team excavated at Elkab, but he would work with the Belgian mission under Capart's successors. Even at an old age he was a daily visitor to the excavation site.

Mond, Robert Ludwig (1867-1938)   No. 162-163

British chemist who succeeded his father as director of the chemicals company Brunner Mond. He took an interest in Egyptian archaeology and financed many archaeological expeditions, including those of the Egypt Exploration Society and the Liverpool Institute of Archaeology. He also directed excavations himself in the Theban necropolis, as well as at Armant. His personal collection of antiquities was bequeathed to the British Museum.

Montet, Pierre (1885-1966)   No. 3

French Egyptologist and professor of Egyptology at the University of Strasbourg and the Collège de France in Paris. He excavated at the site of Byblos in Lebanon, but then returned to Egypt and dedicated most of his career to the archaeological exploration of Tanis, where he made many important discoveries, such as the royal tombs of several kings of the 21st and 22nd Dynasties.

Montu   No. 124, 164-165, 177

Falcon-headed war god who was worshipped mainly in the Theban region, as illustrated by the Montu temples at Karnak, Medamud, Armant and Tod.

Nabawiya Mahmud Ahmed (dates unknown)   No. 175

Youngest daughter of *ghafir* Mahmud Ahmed Ali. According to Jean Capart, she was an independent woman who got married and divorced twice, much to her father's dismay.

Naville, Édouard (1844-1926)   No. 131

Swiss Egyptologist who assisted Karl Richard Lepsius with the publication of the *Denkmäler aus Ägypten und Äthiopien*. He excavated for the Egypt Exploration Fund/Society at many sites in the Delta, but later also in Upper Egypt where he worked for many years at Deir el-Bahari.

Neferirkare (2475-2455 BCE)　　　　　　　　　　　　No. 46-47
Third king of the 5th Dynasty. His pyramid at Abusir was the largest one built during the 5th Dynasty. An important cache of papyri, known as the Abusir Papyri, was found in his mortuary temple; these ancient documents provide insights into the administrative management of an Old Kingdom mortuary temple.

Neferirtenef (c. 2480 BCE)　　　　　　　　　　No. 56-57, 59-61
High official of the 5th Dynasty. His mastaba tomb is located at North Saqqara and was already excavated by Auguste Mariette in the late 1850s and early 1860s. With the financial assistance of Édouard Empain, the funerary chapel of this tomb was reexcavated, dismantled and moved to Brussels, where it was reconstructed in the Egyptian galleries of the museum.

Nefertiti (c. 1380-1340 BCE)　　　　　　　　　　　　No. 92
Principal wife of Akhenaten. Her famous painted limestone bust, now in Berlin, is one of the most iconic works of art, not only of the Amarna period, but of the entire Egyptian civilisation.

Nehri I (c. 1980 BCE)　　　　　　　　　　　　　　　No. 87
Governor of the 15th Upper Egyptian nome, who lived at the end of the 11th to the beginning of the 12th Dynasties and was buried at Deir el-Bersha.

Neith-Hotep (c. 3000 BCE)　　　　　　　　　　　　No. 123
Wife of the 1st Dynasty King Aha. She was probably buried in the so-called 'Royal Tomb' at Naqada, which was initially identified as the tomb of Menes.

Nekhbet　　　　　　　　　　　　　　　　　　No. 176-181
Vulture-goddess who was the principal deity of Elkab. She was also the tutelary goddess of Upper Egypt and, together with the cobra-goddess Wadjet, divine protectress of the pharaoh.

Nemes　　　　　　　　　　　　　　　　　　　　No. 177
Striped cloth headdress worn by the pharaoh as a royal symbol as early as the 1st Dynasty.

Netjeruser (c. 2350 BCE)　　　　　　　　　　　　　No. 58
High official of the 5th Dynasty. He may have been a son of pharaoh Unas. His mastaba was proposed to Jean Capart, who refused it in favour of the mastaba of Neferirtenef. It was later acquired by Edward E. Ayer for the Field Museum of Natural History in Chicago.

Niuserre (2445-2421 BCE)　　　　　　　　　　　　No. 45
Sixth king of the 5th Dynasty. The most prolific builder of his dynasty, he built no less than six pyramid complexes for himself and his family in the necropolis of Abusir.

Nolf, Pierre (1873-1953)　　　　　　　　　　　　No. 144
Belgian physician and politician. He was a professor at the University of Liège and Belgian Minister for the Arts and Sciences between 1922 and 1925. He was also personal physician to the king and queen, and in this capacity joined the royal voyage to Egypt in 1930.

Orban-Viot, Ernest (1866-1909)　　　　　　　　　　No. 93
Belgian photographer who made stereoscopic photos in Egypt, some of which were bequeathed by his son to the photographic archives of the Royal Museums of Art and History in Brussels.

Osiris　　　　　　　　　　　　　　　　No. 106, 133, 139
The god of death, resurrection and fertility, and one of the most important deities in the Egyptian pantheon.

Pendlebury, John Devitt Stringfellow (1904-1941)　　No. 88-91
British archaeologist with a primary interest in Minoan archaeology. He excavated in Crete and succeeded Arthur Evans as director of the excavations at Knossos. He also directed the work of the Egypt Exploration Society at Amarna between 1930 and 1936.

Pepi II (2278-2184 BCE)　　　　　　　　　　　　　No. 193
Penultimate king of the 6th Dynasty and one of the longest reigning monarchs of ancient Egypt, remaining over sixty years on the throne. He suceeded his half-brother Merenre and was buried at South Saqqara.

Per-Ankh　　　　　　　　　　　　　　　　　　No. 88
Temple institution where priests were trained in reading and copying religious and funerary texts. Scribes and children of the Egyptian elite were also educated there.

Petosiris (c. 300 BCE)　　　　　　　　　　　　No. 84-85
High priest of Thoth who lived at the end of the Late Period and beginning of the Ptolemaic Period.

Petrie, William Matthew Flinders (1853-1942)　　No. 66, 118
British Egyptologist who held the first chair in Egyptology in Britain (University College London). He set new standards in excavation methods and recording within Egyptian archaeology, did ground-breaking work at many archaeological sites in Egypt and Palestine, and trained a whole generation of archaeologists and Egyptologists, including Jean Capart who studied under him in 1899.

Pillet, Maurice (1881-1964)　　　　　　　　　　　　No. 154
French archaeologist and architect. He was a member of the Institut Français d'Archéologie Orientale. After the death of Georges Legrain, he directed the work of the Service des Antiquités de l'Égypte at Karnak and continued the excavations and restorations at the Temple of Amun.

Polinet, Paul (dates unknown)   No. 69, 79, 145

Belgian journalist and photographer. An accredited photographer of the royal voyage to Egypt in 1930.

Préaux, Claire (1904-1979)   No. 112

Belgian historian and classical philologist. She was a professor at the Université Libre de Bruxelles and the first female and foreign 'corresponding member' of the French Académie des Inscriptions et Belles-Lettres. Together with Jean Capart, she was one of the driving forces behind the Semaine égyptologique, held in Brussels in 1930. She also received the Francqui Prize (1953), Belgium's highest scientific distinction.

Ptah   No. 64-66

As a creator god, he was one of the oldest gods in the Egyptian pantheon, attested to as early as the 1st Dynasty.

Ptolemy VI (186-145 BCE)   No. 129

Sixth king of the Ptolemaic Period. He was expelled from the throne of Egypt in 164 BCE by his younger brother Ptolemy VIII, but reinstated in 163 BCE.

Quftis   No. 172-174, 186

Specialised labourers from the Upper Egyptian town of Quft. First hired and trained by William Matthew Flinders Petrie, they built up great expertise in excavation techniques. Even today, they continue to work at excavation sites all over Egypt.

Quibell, James Edward (1867-1935)   No. 53, 56-58

British Egyptologist who was trained by William Matthew Flinders Petrie. He discovered the so-called 'Main Deposit' at Hierakonpolis, in which the famous Narmer Palette was found. He also excavated at Elkab in the winter of 1896–1897. As chief inspector at Saqqara for the Service des Antiquités de l'Égypte, he unearthed the mastaba of Neferirtenef, acquired by Jean Capart in 1905–1906.

Qusi (dates unknown)   No. 188

Egyptian sheikh whose tomb is located atop the hill in front of Beit Clarke, the Belgian excavation house at el-Nasrab near Elkab.

Ramesses II (1279-1213 BCE)   No. 65, 76-77, 81, 138-139, 200-201

Third king of the 19th Dynasty. He ruled for an exceptionally long time, leaving behind a vast number of monuments throughout the Egyptian and Nubian Nile Valley.

Ramesses III (1184-1153 BCE)   No. 142-145, 149

Second king of the 20th Dynasty and the New Kingdom's last powerful ruler. He is thought to have been killed following a conspiracy plotted by his wife Tiye (not to be confused with another Tiye, the wife of King Amenhotep III) and the royal harem.

Rawer (c. 2460 BCE)   No. 34

High official who lived during the reign of the 5th Dynasty King Neferirkare. He was buried in a monumental mastaba located in the Central Field Cemetery at Giza.

Re   No. 5

Heliopolitan sun god and one of the most important deities in the Egyptian pantheon.

Reis   No. 13, 166, 171-172, 180, 186

Arabic word meaning 'foreman of the workmen'. During excavations, the *reis* organises the work of the Egyptian labourers, sometimes assisted by one or several overseers.

Rowe, Alan (1890-1968)   No. 69

British Egyptologist and archaeologist. He worked in Palestine and Nubia, but mainly at sites in Egypt. His excavations at the pyramid complex of Snefru at Meidum were visited by Queen Elisabeth of Belgium and Jean Capart during the royal voyage of 1930. Film footage of this excavation, including the royal visit, is kept at the archives of the University of Pennsylvania Museum of Archaeology and Anthropology.[2]

Sais   No. 4

Running footmen who cleared the road for wealthy Egyptians and foreign tourists by running in front of or alongside their horse-drawn carriages.

Saqiya   No. 93, 189

Mechanical water-lifting device comprising a large wooden wheel with attached scoops for drawing water from a source. In rural Egypt, a *saqiya* is usually driven by cattle.

Sayed 'Cid' Mahmud (dates unknown)   No. 6-7, 13

Egyptian workman in Jean Capart's team during the excavations at Heliopolis in 1907. His precise function is not known.

Selim Hassan (1886-1961)   No. 34, 38

Egyptian Egyptologist and the first Egyptian professor of Egyptology at Cairo University. He excavated for nearly ten years in the Giza necropolis and participated in the UNESCO Nubian rescue campaign.

Sema-tawy   No. 104

Symbol of the unification of Upper and Lower Egypt, depicted as the binding of knotted papyrus and reed plants.

Senusret I (1956-1911 BCE)   No. 5, 74

Second king of the 12th Dynasty. He rebuilt the Temple of Re at Heliopolis, which was the largest and most important centre of the sun cult. He launched a military campaign in Lower Nubia and established Egypt's southern border at the Second Cataract.

---

2   This footage can be watched at https://youtu.be/YSsdymy_55g (for the royal visit, see minute 32:59; accessed 19/12/2022).

Senusret III (1870-1831 BCE)   No. 63, 77, 124

Fifth king of the 12th Dynasty. He reinforced Egypt's southern border by constructing a series of fortresses in the area of the Second Cataract. He also built the Temple of Montu at Medamud.

Service des Antiquités de l'Égypte (1858-today)
No. 33, 43, 48, 53-56, 63, 65, 71, 133, 151, 174

Created in 1858 by Auguste Mariette, this institution managed archaeological and Egyptological fieldwork in Egypt. It was initially led by French Egyptologists, up until the appointment in 1953 of Mustafa Amer, its first Egyptian director. It eventually became the Ministry of Tourism and Antiquities, which remains the official governmental body managing and controlling fieldwork in Egypt.

Seshat   No. 104

Goddess of all forms of writing and measuring. She is often depicted as a woman wearing a leopard skin and a headdress with a headband surmounted by an enigmatic symbol representing a rosette or seven-pointed star.

Seti I (1294-1279 BCE)   No. 1, 99, 101, 104-106, 130

Second king of the 19th Dynasty. He was the father of Ramesses II and his reign marked an apex of ancient Egyptian artistic tradition, as illustrated by his magnificent tomb in the Valley of the Kings and especially his temple at Abydos.

Shaduf   No. 119

Irrigation tool used to lift and transfer water between a water source and a canal or basin. It consists of a long wooden pole with a vessel at one end and a weight at the other.

Sheikh   No. 184, 188

Honorific Arabic title that commonly refers to the chief of a tribe. In rural Egypt, the term is also attributed a variety of meanings to designate an important person, from the mayor of a village to someone known to have led a virtuous and pious life.

Snefru (2613-2589 BCE)   No. 63, 67-69

First king of the 4th Dynasty. His three funerary complexes at Meidum and Dahshur are the first attempts in the history of ancient Egyptian architecture to create true rather than step pyramids.

Sobek   No. 70-71, 192

Crocodile god whose main cult centres were at the Temple of Kom Ombo and throughout the Fayum.

Sobekhotep III (c. 1745 BCE)   No. 179

Seventh king of the 13th Dynasty. Fragments of a chapel dedicated to him were found inside the Temple of Nekhbet at Elkab.

Sobekneferu (1777-1773 BCE)   No. 77

Last pharaoh of the 12th Dynasty. She was one of the few women who effectively ruled over ancient Egypt.

Soknopaios   No. 70

Local variety of the god Sobek, attested to in the Fayum.

Stiénon, Jean (1911-1993)   No. 173, 180, 183, 186

Belgian architect who joined Jean Capart's excavation team at Elkab in 1937 and 1938. After the death of Capart in 1947, he co-directed the short Elkab study campaign of February 1949.

Sufragi   No. 17, 23, 184

Arabic word meaning 'house servant'. *Sufragis* saw to the upkeep and other household issues of an excavation house.

Taharqa (690-664 BCE)   No. 149

Fourth king of the 25th Dynasty. He is part of the so-called Kushite Dynasty when Egypt was ruled by a line of Nubian kings.

Tahtib   No. 187

Upper Egyptian folk dance with wooden sticks, which evolved from a stick-fighting martial art, known since ancient Egyptian times.

Talatat   No. 82, 151

Sandstone or limestone blocks from the Amarna period, of standardised size, used for the construction of the Aten Temples at Karnak and Amarna.

Teti (2345-2323 BCE)   No. 47, 51-53, 55

First king of the 6th Dynasty. Like his predecessor Unas, his pyramid at North Saqqara was inscribed with Pyramid Texts. His oldest daughter married the high official Mereruka, whose mastaba tomb lies immediately north of Teti's pyramid.

Thirionet, Marguerite (1878-1955)   No. 37, 40, 42, 70-71, 73-74, 76-77, 81-82, 90, 112-113, 128, 191, 195, front cover

Second wife of Jean Capart. They married in 1913, two years after Capart's first wife Alix Idiers passed away. She made her first trip to Egypt in 1927, when she joined her husband's team at the Tell Hiw excavations. Three more trips would follow, including the Nile cruise of 1930 with the American Goldman family.

Thoth   No. 84, 176, 179, 182

God of writing and knowledge. He is represented as an ibis or a baboon, or as a human figure with the head of those animals.

Thutmose II (1492-1479 BCE)   No. 134

Fourth king of the 18th Dynasty. He was married to his half-sister Hatshepsut who usurped most of his building projects, although several monuments in his name have been identified in the Temple of Amun at Karnak.

Thutmose III (1479-1425 BCE) No. 157, 178, 182
Fifth king of the 18th Dynasty. His expansionist policies resulted in the conquest and annexation of substantial foreign territories, to form the largest empire Egypt has ever seen. His successful military campaigns are recorded in the Temple of Amun at Karnak, and his cartouche was also found on blocks in the Temple of Nekhbet at Elkab.

Ti (c. 2300 BCE) No. 50
High official of the 5th Dynasty. He oversaw the pyramid complexes and sun temples of King Niuserre and some of his predecessors.

Tiye (c. 1410-1340 BCE) No. 146-147
Principal wife of King Amenhotep III and mother of Akhenaten. Many sculptures, such as the one found at Medinet Habu, portray her alongside her husband.

Trajan (98-117) No. 197
Roman emperor of the Nerva-Antonine Dynasty. He was quite active in Egypt and is depicted in offering scenes in different temples, notably the Temple of Hathor at Dendera and his kiosk at Philae.

Tutankhamun (1336-1327 BCE) No. 120, 125-127, 156, 189
Twelfth king of the 18th Dynasty, immediately following the Amarna Period. The discovery of his intact tomb by Howard Carter in 1922 is one of the greatest archaeological finds of all time.

Uraeus No. 177
Symbol for the cobra-goddess Wadjet. In an upright position, it protrudes from most royal crowns and headdresses, usually together with the vulture-goddess Nekhbet, as a symbol of sovereignty and divine royal authority.

Userkaf (2323-2321 BCE) No. 47
First king of the 5th Dynasty. Contrary to his 4th Dynasty predecessors, he returned to Saqqara for the building of his pyramid complex. At Abu Ghurab, he built the first of a series of sun temples that would become characteristic of royal architecture during the 5th Dynasty.

van de Walle, Baudouin (1901-1988) No. 2, 33, 55, 106-109, 159, 192-193
Belgian Egyptologist, student of Jean Capart and one of his closest collaborators, he succeeded Capart at the University of Liège. In 1925, he visited Egypt for the first time and participated the same year in the excavations of the Egypt Exploration Society at the Osireion in Abydos. In 1930, he worked with Robert Mond at the Bucheum in Armant.

Verhoogen, Violette (1898-2001) No. 183, 186-187
Belgian classical philologist and colleague of Jean Capart at the Royal Museums of Art and History, where she was curator for the collections of Greek and Roman antiquities. At Capart's invitation, she joined the Elkab excavations in 1937.

Vyse, Howard (1784-1853) No. 41
British army officer who also excavated in Egypt. His explorations of the Giza pyramids were exceptional, both in terms of the methods employed (gunpowder to dismantle parts of the pyramids) and the published results, which remained of key importance up until modern times. He was also the first to explore the small provincial pyramid at el-Kula, later investigated by Jean Capart and his team in 1945.

Wepwawet No. 102
Jackal-god whose name literally means 'Opener of Ways'. He was a funerary deity associated with mummification, with an important cult centre at Abydos.

Werbrouck, Marcelle (1889-1959)
No. 2, 37, 42, 68, 82, 87, 89-90, 106, 112, 128, 183, 186-187
Belgium's first female Egyptologist. She studied under Jean Capart and became one of his closest collaborators. She succeeded Capart as curator of the Egyptian collection at the Royal Museums of Art and History and as director of the Fondation (now Association) Égyptologique Reine Élisabeth. She participated in the excavations led by Capart at Tell Hiw and Elkab, but also accompanied Capart on many other trips to Egypt. Capart appointed her field director for the excavations at Elkab; however, this was refused by Étienne Drioton, head of the Service des Antiquités de l'Égypte, and Capart was forced to appoint Arpag Mekhitarian instead.

Wesirwer (c. 380-343 BCE) No. 177
High official who lived during the 30th Dynasty. He was mayor of Thebes, a scribe, and a priest of Montu. A statue of him found by Jean Capart at Elkab is now in the Egyptian Museum in Cairo (JE 89121).

Yussef Kamel (1882-1965 ?) No. 107, 111
Grandson of Mohammed Ali, the ruler of Egypt between 1805 and 1848.

Zir No. 16, 20
Arabic word for a terracotta water jar.

Selected Bibliography

PREFACE

- Breasted, John Henry. 1900. *Egypt through the Stereoscope: A Journey through the Land of the Pharaohs*. New York, Underwood & Underwood.
- Bruffaerts, Jean-Michel. 1998. 'Une reine au pays de Toutankhamon'. *Museum Dynasticum* 10: 3–35.
- Bruffaerts, Jean-Michel. 2005. 'Un mastaba égyptien pour Bruxelles'. *Bulletin des Musées royaux d'art et d'histoire* 76: 5–36.
- Bruffaerts, Jean-Michel. 2006. 'Les coulisses d'un voyage royal : Le roi Albert et la reine Elisabeth en Égypte avec Jean Capart (1930)'. *Museum Dynasticum* 18: 28–49.
- Bruffaerts, Jean-Michel. 2022. *Jean Capart : Le chroniqueur de l'Égypte*. Brussels, Racine.
- Bruwier, Marie-Cécile & Doyen, Florence (eds). 2019. *Héliopolis : La ville du soleil*. Brussels, Fondation Boghossian–Villa Empain.
- Capart, Jean. 1901. 'En Égypte: Notes de voyage'. *Annales de la Société d'archéologie de Bruxelles. Mémoires, rapports et documents* 15: 153–181.
- Capart, Jean. 1912. *Abydos : Le temple de Séti Ier : Étude générale*. Brussels, Rossignol & Van den Bril.
- Capart, Jean. 1923. *Toutankhamon*. Brussels, Vromant.
- Capart, Jean. 1927. 'Rapport sur une fouille faite du 14 au 20 Février 1927 dans la nécropole de Héou'. *Annales du Service des Antiquités de l'Égypte* 27: 43–48.
- Capart, Jean. 1928a. 'Communication faite au Congrès des Orientalistes d'Oxford'. *Chronique d'Égypte* 4(7): 18–23.
- Capart, Jean. 1928b. 'Rapport du directeur : Exercice 1927–1928'. *Chronique d'Égypte* 4(7): 2–14.
- Capart, Jean. 1929. 'Mission en Égypte : Janvier–Mars 1929'. *Chronique d'Égypte* 4(8): 189–191.
- Capart, Jean. 1930a. 'Coins ignorés d'Égypte'. *Chronique d'Égypte* 5(10): 180–188.
- Capart, Jean. 1930b. 'Visite officielle du Roi et de la Reine des Belges au Roi d'Égypte'. *Chronique d'Égypte* 5(10): 165–179.
- Capart, Jean. 1932. 'Rapport du directeur : Exercice 1930–1931'. *Chronique d'Égypte* 7(13–14): 1–11.
- Capart, Jean. 1940. 'Assemblée générale : Rapport du directeur'. *Chronique d'Égypte* 15(29): 13–16.
- Capart, Jean. 1946. *Fouilles en Égypte : El Kab, impressions et souvenirs*. Brussels, Fondation Égyptologique Reine Élisabeth.
- Capart, Jean & Werbrouck, Marcelle. 1934. 'Lettres d'Égypte'. *Chronique d'Égypte* 9(18): 225–239.
- Caraffa, Costanza. 2011. 'From "photo libraries" to "photo archives": On the epistemological potential of art-historical photo collections'. In: Caraffa, Constanza (ed.). *Photo Archives and the Photographic Memory of Art History* (Italienische Forschungen des Kunsthistorischen Institutes in Florenz: I Mandorli 14). Berlin, Deutscher Kunstverlag: 11–44.
- De Keyser, Eugénie. 1947. 'Jean Capart professeur et conférencier'. *Chronique d'Égypte* 22(44): 209–210.
- De Meyer, Marleen; Vandersmissen, Jan; Verbruggen, Christophe; Claes, Wouter; Delvaux, Luc; Bruwier, Marie-Cécile; Quertinmont, Arnaud; Warmenbol, Eugène; Bavay Laurent & Willems, Harco. 2019. 'Pyramids and progress: Belgian expansionism and the making of Egyptology, 1830–1952'. In: Navratilova, Hana; Gertzen, Thomas L.; Dodson, Aidan & Bednarski, Andrew (eds). *Towards a History of Egyptology: Proceedings of the Egyptological Section of the 8th ESHS Conference in London, 2018* (Investigatio Orientis 4). Münster, Zaphon: 173–193.
- De Meyer, Marleen; Bruffaerts, Jean-Michel & Vandersmissen, Jan. 2023a. 'The Fondation Égyptologique Reine Élisabeth in Belgium and the creation of national and transnational Egyptological research infrastructures in the 1920–1940s'. In: Matthes, Olaf & Gertzen, Thomas L. (eds). *Oriental Societies & Societal Self-Assertion: Associations, Funds and Societies for the Archaeological Exploration of the 'Ancient Near East'*. Münster, Zaphon.
- De Meyer, Marleen; Claes, Wouter; Mahran, Noha M.A.; Van der Perre, Athena & Gräzer Ohara, Aude. 2023b. 'Working with Capart: Quftis and local workmen during the Elkab excavation seasons, 1937–1946'. In: Navratilova, Hana; Gertzen, Thomas L.; De Meyer, Marleen; Dodson, Aidan M. & Bednarski, Andrew (eds). *Addressing Diversity. Inclusive Histories of Egyptology* (Investigatio Orientis 9). Münster, Zaphon: 339–360.
- Der Manuelian, Peter. 1992. 'George Andrew Reisner on archaeological photography'. *Journal of the American Research Center in Egypt* 29: 1–34.
- Edwards, Elizabeth & Hart, Janice. 2004. 'Photographs as objects'. In: Edwards, Elizabeth & Hart, Janice (eds). *Photographs Objects Histories: On the Materiality of Images*. London, Routledge: 1–15.
- Gräzer Ohara, Aude; Delvaux, Luc; Van der Perre, Athena; De Meyer, Marleen & Claes, Wouter. 2023. 'Jean Capart, Neferirtenef et les mastabas perdus d'Auguste Mariette'. In: Podvin, Jean-Louis & Devauchelle, Didier (eds), *Actes du colloque « Mariette, deux siècles après »*. Boulogne-sur-Mer.
- Gräzer Ohara, Aude; Van der Perre, Athena; De Meyer, Marleen & Claes, Wouter. 2021. 'Un demi-siècle d'égyptologie en images'. *Archéologia* 596: 18–19.
- Greene, John Beasly. 1854. *Le Nil : Monuments, paysages, explorations photographiques*. Paris, Blanquart-Évrard.

- Greene, John Beasly. 1855. *Fouilles exécutées à Thèbes dans l'année 1855 : Textes hiéroglyphiques et documents inédits*. Paris, Firmin-Didot.
- Humphreys, Andrew. 2014. *Grand Hotels of Egypt in the Golden Age of Travel*. Cairo, American University in Cairo Press.
- Humphreys, Andrew. 2015. *On the Nile in the Golden Age of Travel*. Cairo, American University in Cairo Press.
- Hüttner, Michaela. 2016. 'Geschichte der Fotografie: Die ersten 50 Jahre'. In: Haag, Sabine & Hüttner, Michaela (eds). *Von Alexandria nach Abu Simbel: Ägypten in frühen Fotografien*. Vienna, Kunsthistorisches Museum: 11–19.
- Keimer, Ludwig. 1931. 'L'égyptologie et les sciences naturelles'. *Chronique d'Égypte* 6(12) : 306–311.
- Lehnert, Isolde. 2023. 'An independent scholar and collector: Ludwig Keimer in Egypt'. In: Navratilova, Hana; Gertzen, Thomas L.; De Meyer, Marleen; Dodson, Aidan & Bednarski, Andrew (eds). *Addressing Diversity. Inclusive Histories of Egyptology* (Investigatio Orientis 9). Münster, Zaphon: 73–108.
- Limme, Luc. 2008. 'Elkab, 1937–2007: Seventy years of Belgian archaeological research'. *British Museum Studies in Ancient Egypt and Sudan* 9: 15–50.
- McFayden, Lesley & Hicks, Dan (eds). 2020. *Archaeology and Photography: Time, Objectivity and Archive*. London, Bloomsbury.
- Petrie, William Matthew Flinders. 1904. *Methods and Aims in Archaeology*. London, Macmillan.
- Piacentini, Patrizia. 2014. 'Theodor Kofler et les premières photographies aériennes des monuments égyptiens'. *Bulletin de la Société française d'Égyptologie* 190: 23–36.
- Piacentini, Patrizia (ed.). 2015. *Egitto dal cielo, 1914: La riscoperta del fotografo pioniere, prigioniero, professionista Theodor Kofler / Egypt from the sky, 1914: The Rediscovery of the Photographer Pioneer, Prisoner, Professional Theodor Kofler*. Firenze, Phasar Edizioni.
- Rammant-Peeters, Agnes (ed.). 1994. *Palmen en tempels: Fotografie in Egypte in de XIXe eeuw / La photographie en Égypte au XIXe siècle / 19th-century Photography in Egypt*. Leuven, Peeters.
- Sontag, Susan. 1977. *On Photography*. London, Penguin Books.
- Van der Perre, Athena; Claes, Wouter; De Meyer, Marleen & Gräzer Ohara, Aude. 2021. 'Sura-project: Het ontstaan van de Belgische Egyptologie in beeld'. *Ta-Mery* 14: 88–111.
- Van Loo, Anne & Bruwier, Marie-Cécile (eds). 2010. *Héliopolis*. Brussels, Fonds Mercator.
- Vanhulle, Dorian. 2023. *Une ancienne collection royale aux Musées royaux d'Art et d'Histoire de Bruxelles : Les antiquités égyptiennes du roi Léopold II* (Orientalia Lovaniensia Analecta). Leuven, Peeters.
- Werbrouck, Marcelle. 1947. 'Jean Capart et la Fondation Égyptologique Reine Élisabeth'. *Chronique d'Égypte* 22(44): 192–196.
- Werbrouck, Marcelle. 1949. 'Assemblée générale 8 octobre 1848 : Rapport de la directrice'. *Chronique d'Égypte* 24(47): 5–9.
- Yelles, Anissa. 2020. *Aux origines de la photographie archéologique : De Rome en Afrique* (Archives et histoire de l'archéologie 3). Drémil-Lafage, Mergoil.

BELGIAN EGYPTOLOGY

- Bavay, Laurent; Bruwier, Marie-Cécile; Claes, Wouter & De Strooper, Ingrid (eds). 2012. *Ceci n'est pas une pyramide… : Un siècle de recherche archéologique belge en Égypte*. Leuven, Peeters.
- Brasseur, Anne-Marie & Capart, Auguste. 1974. *Jean Capart ou le rêve comblé de l'égyptologie*. Brussels, Arts & Voyages.
- Bruffaerts, Jean-Michel. 1999. 'Arpag Mekhitarian'. In: Cannuyer, Christian; Mawet, Francine & Ries, Julien (eds). *Le ciel dans les civilisations orientales* (Acta orientalia Belgica 12). Brussels, Société belge d'études orientales: xiii–xviii.
- Bruffaerts, Jean-Michel. 2013. 'Bruxelles, capitale de l'égyptologie : Le rêve de Jean Capart'. In: Bickel, Susanne; Fischer-Elfert, Hans-Werner; Loprieno, Antonio & Richter, Sebastian (eds). *Ägyptologen und Ägyptologien zwischen Kaiserreich und Gründung der beiden deutschen Staaten: Reflexionen zur Geschichte und Episteme eines altertumswissenschaftlichen Fachs im 150. Jahr der Zeitschrift für ägyptische Sprache und Altertumskunde* (Zeitschrift für ägyptische Sprache und Altertumskunde. Beiheft 1). Berlin, Akademie Verlag: 193–241.
- Bruffaerts, Jean-Michel. 2018. 'Marcelle Werbrouck ou l'égyptologie belge au féminin'. In: Doyen, Florence; Preys, René & Quertinmont, Arnaud (eds). *Sur le chemin du Mouseion d'Alexandrie : Études offertes à Marie-Cécile Bruwier* (Les Cahiers Égypte Nilotique et Méditérranéenne 19). Montpellier, ENIM: 43–71.
- Bruffaerts, Jean-Michel. 2022. *Jean Capart : Le chroniqueur de l'Égypte*. Brussels, Racine.
- De Meyer, Marleen & de Cartier d'Yves, Sibille (eds). 2020. *Belgians on the Nile: A History of royal Visits, Entrepreneurship, and Archaeological Exploration in Egypt*. Alexandria, Bibliotheca Alexandrina.
- Delvaux, Luc (ed.). 2023. *Expédition Égypte : Histoires d'une collection*. Brussels, Ludion.
- Mekhitarian, Arpag. 1989. 'Dans l'intimité de Baudouin van de Walle (21.10.1901–26.12.1988)'. *Chronique d'Égypte* 64 (127/128): 5–15.
- Urbain, Sophie; Quertinmont, Arnaud & Bruwier, Marie-Cécile (eds). 2020. *Made in Belgium: Industriels belges en Égypte (1830–1952)*. Morlanwelz, Musée royal de Mariemont.
- Van Loo, Anne & Bruwier, Marie-Cécile (eds). 2010. *Héliopolis*. Brussels, Fonds Mercator.

INTERNATIONAL EGYPTOLOGY

- Bèche-Wittmann, Marie & Bouilloc, Christine (eds). 2021. *L'Égypte de Marcelle Baud 1890–1987 : L'archéologie au féminin & en dessins*. Clermont-Ferrand, Bleu Autour.
- Bednarski, Andrew; Dodson, Aidan & Ikram, Salima (eds). 2021. *A History of World Egyptology*. Cambridge, Cambridge University Press.
- Bierbrier, Morris L. (ed.) 2019. *Who Was Who in Egyptology*. London, The Egypt Exploration Society (5th revised edition).
- Colla, Elliott. 2008. *Conflicted Antiquities: Egyptology, Egyptomania, Egyptian Modernity*. Durham, Duke University Press.
- Navratilova, Hana; Gertzen, Thomas L.; Dodson, Aidan & Bednarski, Andrew (eds). 2019. *Towards a History of Egyptology: Proceedings of the Egyptological Section of the 8th ESHS Conference in London, 2018* (Investigatio Orientis 4). Münster, Zaphon.
- Navratilova, Hana; Gertzen, Thomas L.; De Meyer, Marleen; Dodson, Aidan & Bednarski, Andrew (eds). 2023. *Addressing Diversity: Inclusive Histories of Egyptology* (Investigatio Orientis 9). Münster, Zaphon.
- Quirke, Stephen. 2010. *Hidden Hands: Egyptian Workforces in Petrie Excavation Archives, 1880–1924*. Bristol, Bristol Classical Press.
- Reid, Donald Malcolm. 2002. *Whose Pharaohs? Archaeology, Museums, and Egyptian National Identity from Napoleon to World War I*. Berkeley, University of California Press.
- Reid, Donald Malcolm. 2015. *Contesting Antiquity in Egypt: Archaeologies, Museums, and the Struggle for Identities from World War I to Nasser*. Cairo, American University in Cairo Press.
- Thompson, Jason. 2015–2018. *Wonderful Things: A History of Egyptology*. 3 volumes. Cairo, American University in Cairo Press.

HISTORIC IMAGES IN EGYPT AND NUBIA

- Azim, Michel & Réveillac, Gérard. 2004. *Karnak dans l'objectif de Georges Legrain : Catalogue raisonné des archives photographiques du premier directeur des travaux de Karnak de 1895 à 1917*. Paris, CNRS éditions.
- Berman, Lawrence Michael. 2018. *Unearthing Ancient Nubia: Photographs from the Harvard University–Boston Museum of Fine Arts Expedition*. Boston, Museum of Fine Arts.
- Claes, Wouter; De Meyer, Marleen; Van der Perre, Athena & Gräzer Ohara, Aude. 2023. '« Si mes photos sont bien réussies, on verra une merveille » : Jean Capart et sa collection photographique à Bruxelles'. *Les nouvelles de l'archéologie* 170 : 20–25.
- Driaux, Delphine & Arnette, Marie-Lys. 2016. *Instantanés d'Égypte*. Cairo, Institut français d'archéologie orientale du Caire.
- Haag, Sabine & Hüttner, Michaela (eds). 2016. *Von Alexandria nach Abu Simbel: Ägypten in frühen Fotografien*. Vienna, Kunsthistorisches Museum.
- Larson, John A. 2006. *Lost Nubia: A Centennial Exhibition of Photographs from the 1905–1907 Egyptian Expedition of the University of Chicago*. (University of Chicago. Oriental Institute Museum Publications 24). Chicago, University of Chicago Oriental Institute.
- Riggs, Christina. 2019. *Photographing Tutankhamun: Archaeology, Ancient Egypt, and the Archive*. Cairo, American University in Cairo Press.
- Van der Perre, Athena; Claes, Wouter; De Meyer, Marleen & Gräzer Ohara, Aude. 2022. 'Sura-project: Het ontstaan van de Belgische Egyptologie in beeld'. *Ta-Mery* 14: 88–111.

SURA is a joint research project between the Royal Museums of Art and History in Brussels and the research group Archaeology: Egyptology of KU Leuven. The project is financed by Belspo, the Belgian Science Policy Office, in the framework of the BRAIN-be 2.0 research program (research grant B2/191/P2/SURA).

This research would not have been possible without the assistance, advice and support of many people and institutions. We warmly thank Gunther De Wit (Snoeck Publishers) and Alexandra De Poorter (RMAH) for their proficient coordination of this book project. We thank the SURA follow-up committee for their support the past two years: Els Angenon (RMAH), Laurent Bavay (Université Libre de Bruxelles), Luc Delvaux (RMAH), Peter Der Manuelian (Harvard University), and Carolien Van Zoest (Netherlands Institute for the Near East).

At the RMAH, many colleagues have assisted us throughout different phases of our research. For their expert help in the museum archives of the RMAH, we are grateful to Lee Mouton, Sylvie Paesen, Denis Perin and Gerrit Verhoeven, as well as to our colleagues of the EOS-funded project 'Pyramids and Progress: Belgian expansionism and the making of Egyptology, 1830–1952', in particular Mathieu Geeraerts, Noortje Lambrichts and Joffrey Lienart. The e-Collections team of the RMAH, and in particular Els Angenon and Amélie D'Hoen, are thanked for their help in publishing the photographs in Carmentis, the online collection catalogue of the RMAH.

Our sincere thanks also goes to Jean-Pierre De Cuyper and Joan Vandekerckhove of the Digitisation Facility of the Royal Observatory of Belgium for digitising the glass negatives, and to Els Angenon and Nacha Van Steen of the e-Collections department of the RMAH for coordinating this.

For the translation of the introductory chapter into Arabic, we thank Moussa Al Houchi, as well as Ferida Jawad and Adel Abdelmonein (Netherlands-Flemish Institute in Cairo) for proofreading it.

For help with the identification of the photos, supplying various types of information and stimulating discussions, we thank Jean-Michel Bruffaerts (Fonds Capart), Marie-Cécile Bruwier (Musée royal de Mariemont), Luc Delvaux (RMAH), Peter Der Manuelian (Harvard University), Wendy Doyon (Abydos Archaeology), Annelie Campion, Patrice Le Guilloux, Isolde Lehnert (DAIK), Julie Marchand (RMAH/ULB), Ilona Regulski (British Museum), Joanne Rowland (University of Edinburgh) and Alexandra Van Puyvelde (RMAH).

Published on the occasion of the exhibition *Expedition Egypt* at the Art and History Museum, Brussels, from 31 March until 1 October 2023.

Authors	Aude Gräzer Ohara, Athena Van der Perre, Marleen De Meyer, Wouter Claes
Copy-editing	Mike Goeden
Proofreading	Aude Gräzer Ohara, Athena Van der Perre, Marleen De Meyer, Wouter Claes
Translation into Arabic	Moussa Al Houchi
Proofreading of the Arabic	Ferida Jawad, Adel Abdelmonein
Publications manager RMAH	Alexandra De Poorter
Graphic Design	Keppie & Keppie
Colour separation	Steurs, Wijnegem

Printed at Printer Trento, Italy

ISBN 978 94 616 1776 7
D/2023/0012/13

© all authors and photographers, 2023
© Snoeck Publishers, Ghent, 2023 www.snoeckpublishers.be
© Royal Museums of Art and History, Brussels, 2023 www.kmkg-mrah.be

All rights reserved. No part of this publication may be reproduced or transmitted in any form or by any means, electronic or mechanical, including photocopy, recording or any other information storage and retrieval system, without prior permission in writing from the publisher. Every effort has been made to contact copyright-holders of illustrations. Any copyright-holders whom we have been unable to reach or to whom inaccurate acknowledgment has been made are invited to contact the publisher.